MW01106596

Awakening the Sleeping Giant

BILLY RAY DRIVER

authorHOUSE®

AuthorHouse™
1663 Liberty Drive
Bloomington, IN 47403
www.authorhouse.com
Phone: 1 (800) 839-8640

Published by AuthorHouse 09/14/2018

ISBN: 978-1-5462-5914-5 (sc)
ISBN: 978-1-5462-5913-8 (hc)
ISBN: 978-1-5462-5912-1 (e)

Library of Congress Control Number: 2018910796

Print information available on the last page.

I pray that this book will be comforting and encouraging to all who read it, as God has encouraged me to write this book (2 Corinthians 1:3–4). First of all, I have to give God, who is the Father of our Lord, Jesus Christ, and the Holy Spirit, praise for inspiring me to write this book. The Father of compassion and the God of all comfort, who comforts us in all troubles so that we can comfort those who are experiencing any troubles with the comfort I've received from God. Just as the Holy Spirit inspired me to write this book, I pray that when you read this book that you will be jolted in the Spirit to do what God has purposed for you to do in Jesus's name. In this book I hope to answer the following questions: Why are churches allowing too much complacency and settling for mediocrity? Why is the church choosing not to get out of its comfort zone and staying contented to where it is?

God wants to snatch His people out of their comfort zones because we have become too complacent. God is telling us to awaken in Jesus's name from our complacency. If the church wants to have a great awakening, then we have to allow the Holy Spirit to have free course and start listening again to what the Holy Spirit is saying. If the church refuses to be awakening and chooses to stay in its comfort zone, then God will respect its decision. We have free will and God will not force Himself on anyone. We have to get to the point and say enough is enough and cry out to God: *God help me to get out of my comfort zone. God I do not want to allow complacency dictating me any longer by telling me that it's okay to stay asleep in Sin Dungeon. I want Your will to be done in my life and not my will. I want to get out of satan sleep in Sin Dungeon. I refuse to be his slave in his sleep in Sin Dungeon any longer. I choose to silent the voice of the enemy over my life. God revive me. God, If*

You do not allow the Holy Spirit to stir up a great revival in Your people to cause a great awakening, then we will not be revived.

If you do not know, then you should know that the church is His people and not a building. It is sad to say, but the church has returned back to its vomit. We have allowed the care of this world to creep inside the body of Christ. The church is dealing with divorces, abortions, drug addictions, pornography, greed, lying, hatred, sexual immorality, lasciviousness, and the list goes on and on. God didn't call the church back into bondage or captivity. He has called us out of bondage and captivity. While under the devil sleep in sin spell, the church has allowed innocent unborn babies to die in their mothers' wombs, removal of prayer out of the schools, and now we are allowing guns to replace the Bible in those same schools. The schools have become a war zone instead of a learning zone. God has called the church out of darkness into His marvelous light. "That the creation itself will be set free from its bondage to corruption and obtain the freedom of the glory of the children of God" (Romans 8:21). God doesn't want His creation to stay in bondage. "For God has not called us for impurity, but in holiness" (1 Thessalonians 4:7). He wants us to obtain freedom in His glory according to His Word. "The Spirit of the Lord is upon Me, because He has anointed Me to proclaim good news to the poor. He has sent Me to proclaim liberty to the captives and recovering of sight to the blind, to set at liberty those who are oppressed" (Luke 4:18). He didn't anoint the church back into captivity for satan to control you. He called us to proclaim good news to the poor and liberty to those who are oppressed by the Devil. But the church cannot help anyone if it is living in that sleep in Sin Dungeon along with the world. God wants His people to be awakening before the Second Coming of Jesus Christ. He doesn't want us to be like those five foolish virgins, which I will discuss later on in the book. He wants His people to be awakening before it's too late. While the church is in the sleep in Sin Dungeon, it's impossible to do the will of the Father. God doesn't want to hear, "Lord, Lord did we not prophesy in Your name and cast out demons in Your name and do mighty works in your name." "Not everyone who says to me, 'Lord, Lord,' will enter the kingdom of heaven, but the one who does the will of My Father who is in heaven. On that day many will say to me, 'Lord, Lord, did we not prophesy in Your name, and cast out demons in Your name, and do many mighty works in

Your name?' And then will I declare to them, 'I never knew you; depart from Me, you workers of lawlessness'" (Matthew 7:21–23). If you are doing all those things for your personal glorification, then that is your reward. God wants us to have a personal relationship with Him by believing that Jesus is the Son of God and inviting His Holy Spirit to reside in you. It's hard for the religious and nonbelievers to accept that the trinity consists of God the Father, the Son, Jesus Christ, and the Holy Spirit because They are one. It is hard for religious and nonbelievers to accept that God clothed Himself in human flesh, died on the cross for our sins, and rose from the grave with all resurrection power. It's hard for religious people to believe in the trinity God the Father, Jesus Christ the Son, and the Holy Spirit. It's hard for even the religious people to believe that Jesus is the way, the truth, and the life. Do you not know that you can grieve the Holy Spirit? I'll be discussing how you can grieve the Holy Spirit by rejecting Him in detail in this book. "Or do you not know that your body is a temple of the Holy Spirit within you, whom you have from God? You are not your own" (1 Corinthians 6:19). The church needs to start repossessing its job, its health, its marriages, its children, its mind, its ministry, its lands, and its lives. Mandy Hale (www.planetofsuccess.com/blog/2017/mandy-hale-quotes/ from 65 Inspirational Mandy Hale Quotes #4) said, "Sometimes it takes a heartbreak to shake us awake and help us see we are worth so much more than we're settling for."

To Anita, the love of my life, you mean everything to me.
You are a mighty woman of valor.
You are wise and beautiful on the inside and out.
I am blessed beyond measure to have you at my side.

Contents

Part Four
Robbing God

Part Five
Infirmity Spirit

Part Six
The Great Awakening

Foreword

First, I would like to thank our Lord and Savior Jesus Christ for impressing upon Minister Billy Driver's heart to write such a timely and courageous book to the church in this hour. I have known Minister Driver all his life and have found him, especially in the last forty-something years, to be a man who loves God and God's people. He has been found to be faithful to the Lord, to his family, and to ministries. I have observed him to grow in the revelation of God's Word and in the knowledge of God's church, awakening and arising to be a light in a dark time for our nation and much of the world. Now is the time to be a generation of people radically committed to Jesus Christ so the church can be awakened in order to change this world.

Minister Driver, I believe, has a special anointing and the wisdom to put awesome and powerful words together to help enlighten and equip the body of Christ to arise and fulfill our God-given destiny. This book will challenge the church to examine its own heart to see if they are under the devil's deep-sleep-in-sin spell. This book is powerful and will jolt the church of the Lord Jesus Christ out of her slumbering state. People often can be in such a lethargic state that they fail to realize it and do not know how to be awakened. I believe Minister Driver's book will help the church see that if we keep sleeping in sin, politicians and governments will continue to lead the way. That should not happen, for God has called and commissioned the church to lead mankind to the light in Jesus the Christ.

Minister Driver's book reveals that the church is the sleeping giant and is in need of being awakened out of her slumber and sin. It's imperative that the church realize that God's plans include being vigilantes and sober to the schemes of the enemy. The church has been trapped inside a Sin Enchantment Forest and has forgotten that we have internal resurrection power to help us awaken. This book was written to help the church realize that she has been sleeping far too long and that it is time to awaken to our God-given assignment. Minister Driver takes you down the road of how to awaken in Jesus's name. However, the devil does not want God's people to awaken and be "on" one accord, because this is when the church will impact this world. The Lord wants to pour out His Spirit on all flesh and set the captive free. The church must arise and tell a dying world that Jesus is the answer to sin. This book asks some challenging questions that the church needs to answer, such as why the church loves complacency and its comfort zone. If you have ever wondered why the church is in such a state, this book will reveal just that. This book is a must-have for every believer.

Belinda McCain
Prophet, Pastor, Evangelist, Author of *By His Spirit*

PART ONE

The Sleep in Sin

~ ONE ~

Enchantment Sleep in Sin Forest

Do you recall the story "Rip Van Winkle," by Washington Irving? Rip Van Winkle went to sleep before the American War of Independence and woke up twenty years later. A loyal subject of the British monarch, he went to sleep to escape his nagging wife. But when he woke up, he found that his wife had died, his friends were nowhere to be found, and the British monarch was no longer of any importance in his land. To Van Winkle, these dramatic changes seemed to have happened overnight. How does this story relate to the church today? The church, which is a people—not a building or a place—is sleeping in sin today.

Christianity was founded in the United States during the early colonial period by the Pilgrims, who brought it with them when they fled religious persecution in Europe. According to Wikipedia, there are nearly 280 million Christians, making Christianity the largest religion in the world. The author do not believe that Christianity should never be considered a religion, because Christianity is a God doing and religion is a man doing. According to an ABC News poll, 83 percent of Americans identify as Christians. Most of the rest, 13 percent, profess no religion.[2] If this is the case, why aren't Christians making a difference in the United States? Only fifty people were surveyed for this poll, so it probably isn't an accurate representation of the United States population.

Sleep can be defined as the state of an animal during hibernation, a state of torpid inactivity resembling sleep, or a trance or coma. The devil has put the church into a sleep-in-sin trance, and the church doesn't even know it. The church knows something is wrong, but it cannot escape this

1

trance. Rip Van Winkle, who tried to escape reality by sleeping, found that the world had changed when he finally woke up. The story of Rip Van Winkle sounds much like the church today. Is the church trying to hide its head in the sand, hoping that the evil things happening around us will just go away? Our world is moving in a direction that we don't want it to go, but the church refuses to wake up from the sleep in sin. We are heading toward a collision like a runaway train. We see children shot in our schools and people gunned down in the streets because of the color of their skin. We see sexual immorality running rampant, human trafficking, and children sold into the sex trade, because of lust, greed and the heart of man. We see drug overdoses increasing because the flesh just cannot be satisfied, and our children are committing suicide.

So, you ask, how does this relate to Christianity? Good question. Christians are being lulled into an enchanted sleep in Sin Forest by satan without their consent or knowledge. The Bible tells us that God's people are perishing because of lack of knowledge. By this happening the following devastation has been introduced into the United States: One of the first signs was Roe v. Wade. Roe v. Wade came on the scene while we were under the sleep-in-sin trance of satan in 1973 where the Supreme Court ruled in favor of Roe, who was single and having sex outside of marriage and got pregnant. Now, who was the president at the time during the Roe v. Wade trial? A Republican named Richard Nixon. Roe admitted that she didn't want the baby. She wanted to abort her baby. She claimed that her life wasn't endangered. She didn't want the unborn baby. The baby was a human being at the time of conception. Here are some statistics from the outcome of Roe v. Wade. Ever since the Roe v. Wade ruling, more than 58 million unborn children have lost their lives in their mothers' wombs because of lack of knowledge. Jane Roe, who has since become a vocal, passionate leader in the pro-life movement, challenged abortion regulations and won the court decision. Ever since then, more than 48 million unborn children have ceased to exist in this world. In 2005 alone, there were 1.2 million abortions in the United States. One court decision, instigated by one person, changed the fate and face of generations who have never had the chance to cure cancer, create art and literature, discover energy-conserving innovations, or advance the population of a freedom-loving nation.[3]

In its report titled *Abortion Incidence and Service Availability in the United States, 2011*, the Guttmacher Institute, originally founded as a research affiliate of Planned Parenthood, reported that for 2011, there were 1.05 million abortions in the United States—550,000 fewer than the peak of 1.6 million in 1990.[4] I believe that abortion numbers are declining because of the morning-after pill.

The total number of abortions, since Roe v. Wade in 1973, is 60,069,971. This is based on the numbers reported by the Guttmacher Institute (GI) 1973–2014, with projections of 926,190 for 2015–17. GI has estimated possible undercounts of 3 to 5 percent, so an additional 3 percent is factored into the overall total.[5]

According to the National Pro-Life Alliance, abortion is the leading cause of death in the United States every year, with more than 1.6 million abortions performed on average per year. Those unborn children might have grown up to be doctors or scientists who found a cure for cancer or AIDS, or one of them could have easily became the president of the United States.

Abortions are a tragic within itself, partly because of the devastating remorse, guilt, and condemnation that follow. If you have been a victim of this tragedy, I don't condemn you. God is your judge, not me. The Bible tells us in 1 John 1:9, "If we confess our sins, He is faithful and just [righteous] to forgive us and to cleanse us from all unrighteousness [our sins]." That is the kind of God we serve—a merciful God. I believe that if you have confessed your sins, God has forgiven you and those sins have been thrown into the sea of forgetfulness. Isaiah 43:25 says, "I am He who blots out your transgressions for My own sake, and I will not remember your sins."

As the Lord said to Moses, "Whoever takes a human life shall surely be put to death" (Leviticus 2:17). God is long range, so He knew that we couldn't hold up our end of the bargain. That is why He sent His Son Jesus. It is up to you to walk in forgiveness, not in condemnation. I beseech you to allow your past sins and shame to be used as a stepping-stone to help others, rather than as a stumbling block. We do not have the power to go back and change the past, but our omnipotent God does. According to the Word of God, "As far as the east is from the west, so far does he remove our transgressions from us" (Psalm 103:12 ESV). It's difficult for us to forgive ourselves, because of guilt and condemnation. We don't know how to turn off that lying devil's voice in our minds. The devil comes to kill, steal, and destroy, but Jesus came to give us life—and life more abundantly. Jesus is not surprised by our sins.

We're supposed to help other people get out of their cocoons by telling them about Jesus and what He saved us from. A wise person will learn from someone else's testimony and then not make those same mistakes. Proverb 12:15 says, "The way of a fool is right in his own eyes, but a wise man listens to advice." It is imperative for teenagers and adults to learn from other people's mistakes. Because you belong to Jesus, the life-giving Spirit has given you freedom from the sin that leads to death. Romans 8:1–2 says, "There is therefore no condemnation for those who are in Christ Jesus. For the law of the Spirit of life has set you free in Christ Jesus from the law of sin and death." Jesus said that He came to save the world and not to condemn it. Remember that the law brought sin and death, but Jesus brings life. Can I get an amen?

Romans 8:3–4 says, "For God has done what the law, weakened by the flesh, could not do. By sending His own Son in the likeness of sinful flesh and for sin, He condemned sin in the flesh, in order that the righteous requirement of the law might be fulfilled in us, who walk not according to the flesh but according to the Spirit." God saw that sin keeps us separated from Him, so He sent His Son, Jesus, to condemn sin in the flesh once and for all:

> *So those who live according to the flesh set their minds on the things of the flesh, but those who live according to the Spirit set their minds on the things of the Spirit. For to set the mind on the flesh is death, but to set the mind on the Spirit is life and peace. For the mind set on the flesh is hostile to God, for it does not submit to God's law; indeed, it cannot. Those who are in the flesh cannot please God. You, however, are not in the flesh but in the Spirit, if in fact the Spirit of God dwells in you. Anyone who does not have the Spirit of Christ does not belong to Him. But if Christ is in you, although the body is dead because of sin, the Spirit is life because of righteousness. If the Spirit of Him who raised Jesus from the dead dwells in*

*you, He who raised Christ Jesus from the dead will also give
life to your mortal bodies through His Spirit who dwells in
you. (Romans 8:5–11)*

If you continue to not be awakened by the Holy Spirit, you will
continue to be a puppet to the devil and your flesh, which will keep you
stuck in the enchantment sleep in Sin Forest forever. So please walk in
the Spirit, so that you won't continue to fulfill the lust of the flesh. If
you continue to walk in the flesh, don't be surprised to see such things as
your children misbehaving, divorce becoming more widespread, sexual
immorality and perversion out of control, and addictions running rampant.

According to Merriam-Webster, Inc. dictionary on the Apple I-Tune
App dated 2018, the verb *enchant* means to cast a spell over or bewitch
someone or something. To be *enchanted* means to be enthralled, captivated,
beguiled, engrossed, or hypnotized. Paul wrote in Galatians 3:1, "O foolish
Galatians! Who has bewitched you? It was before your eyes that Jesus
Christ was publicly portrayed as crucified." Although they had previously
walked in the Spirit, the Galatians later allowed their flesh to be perfected
and let the devil get a stronghold in their lives. Without even knowing it,
they fell asleep under the devil's sleep-in-sin trance and became complacent
about the things of this world.

Now the church has become bewitched. O foolish church, who has
bewitched you? I hope the church knows that it is the devil who has
bewitched it and made it complacent. It is the devil's good fortune for
the church to remain in sin sleep. It's easy to go into the devil's enchanted
forest and get trapped in sin sleep, like a bug caught in a Venus flytrap,
especially if you are walking in the flesh. The flesh will take you back to
places where you thought you would never return. In Galatians 1:3, Paul
tells the churches of Galatia about the forest of enchantment, which is like
eating the forbidden fruit. Once you have bitten into it, your flesh will
crave for more and more, until it cannot get satisfied.

You know what your forbidden fruit is—your weaknesses and
vulnerabilities. Once you have tasted the forbidden fruit and experienced
that first high, you'll try again and again to re-create that feeling, just like
a drug addict, but you can't reach that pinnacle again. That's why some
people overdose on drugs because they are trying to mimic that ecstasy

or sensation again and they cannot get that feeling again. Don't continue to be lulled into the devil's enchanted forest, because when he is finished with you, he will make your life miserable by trying to destroy everything important to you—your health, family, friends, job, finances, and the church you attend.

Pornography is another example of sleeping in sin in the enchanted forest after tasting the forbidden fruit. In the computer age, we have personal electronic devices that give us easy access to pornography. Once you look upon that forbidden fruit, however, you'll crave more and never be satisfied. I struggle with this forbidden fruit every day. That's why I have to walk in the Spirit so that I won't continue to fulfill the lust of the flesh. The flesh is weak, but the Spirit is strong. Similarly, once your lips have tasted the forbidden fruit of alcohol, it's difficult to stop. Sex outside of marriage is one of the worst forbidden fruits because it's like a wildfire out of control and you want more and more. You find yourself trapped, sleeping in sin in the enchanted forest with no way of escaping. The list goes on and on, including such sins as addictions to working and shopping. The Bible tells us to flee from these lustful things, which are like indulging our appetites at smorgasbords or buffets. They are intoxicating to our flesh and we cannot get enough.

God does not want you to stay trapped in the sleep in Sin Dungeon. Once you have tasted that the Lord is good, you don't want to stay in the forest of enchantment sleeping in sin any longer. God wants you to rise above those addictions, and He said that if you seek Him, you'll find Him. "Seek ye first the Kingdom of God and His righteousness and all these things shall be added unto you." God doesn't want you to seek after fleshly things. Tell your crazy flesh to get back on that cross where it belongs, each and every day, because the flesh wants to remain in control. But your life is not your own, because you have been bought by the blood of the lamb, Jesus Christ. John 3:16 says, "For God so loved the world, that He gave His only Son, that whoever believes in Him should not perish but have eternal life." Isn't that good news?

Do you realize that the church has been sleeping for more than forty-five years, ever since the Roe v. Wade case? The church is still sleeping deeply in sin, because we have allowed prayer and the Word of God to be taken out of the schools. We have allowed religion to become the norm instead of having a personal relationship with Jesus Christ.

The church has taken its flesh off the cross and revitalized it again. We must tell our harebrained flesh to get back on that cross where it belongs. No flesh will dwell in God's presence. Jesus's flesh was nailed to a cross over two thousand years ago, so speaking the name of Jesus causes the enemy to flee. And the blood of Jesus, which was shed for you and me, is our road map to salvation and forgiveness of sin. There is no remission of sin without the shedding of blood. (Read Hebrews 9:22.) No one can come to the Father except through Jesus, because Jesus is the only bridge to the Father. "Jesus said to him, "I am the way, and the truth, and the life. No one comes to the Father except through Me" (John 14:6).

In John 14:5, Jesus answers Thomas's question, but all the disciples are asking Jesus questions because they aren't sure where He's going. If you are in the enchantment sleep in Sin Forest, you will ask questions such as, "How can we know the way?" The enemy does not want you to know the way to the Father. He wants you to remain blind and ignorant. The enemy wants you to live in the enchantment of Sin Forest forever with him. If you remain in the enchanted forest, your flesh and the enemy will remain in control. You'll think that everything is okay, but it will be obvious that nothing is real. But if you experience the awakening and see the enemy for what he is—a cunning, slimy, little snake—then you will tell that old devil to get back under your feet where he belongs. Then you will see that Jesus is the only way to the Father.

You need to tell the devil to go to hell where he belongs and leave your family alone. Serpents can be word curses and generation curses, but Jesus has given us the authority to trample over them both and denounce them in His name. The devil has no authority over you except what you give him. Denounce word and generation curses simply by saying this:

> Father, I am your child and I speak blessings over my life, my children, and my family. In Jesus's name, I break every generational and word curse that has been spoken over my life, my children, and my family. Father, you have given me dominion and authority on this earth, and I bind the devil's curses. The devil is the prince of lies, and I take

> authority over every lie that has been spoken over my life,
> my children, and my family. As of today, I silence the voice
> of the enemy in Jesus's name. Amen!

Luke 10:19 says, "Behold, I have given you authority to tread on serpents and scorpions and over all the power of the enemy, and nothing shall hurt you." This scripture is talking about the devil, our enemy. Do not misinterpret this verse and literally walk on serpents and scorpions, because you will get bitten or stung. Do not ever tempt the Lord your God.

The devil's only power is the power you give him by staying trapped in the enchantment sleep in Sin Forest. Second Corinthians 11:3 says, "But I am afraid that as the serpent deceived Eve by his cunning, your thoughts will be led astray from a sincere and pure devotion of Christ." If the enemy can trick Eve into eating the forbidden fruit from the Tree of the Knowledge of Good and Evil, he can trick you into eating the forbidden fruit. The devil will try to trick you into thinking that Jesus is not the only way to the Father. Religion is not the way—just ask the Pharisees and Sadducees, hypothetically speaking. Jesus redeemed us from all curses, including word curses. "Christ redeemed us from the curse of the law by becoming a curse for us—for it is written, Cursed is everyone who is hanged on a tree" (Galatians 3:13 ESV).

Are you a member of the chosen generation or the asleep-in-sin generation? If you continue to sleep in sin, then you can expect the following:

1) Divorces within the church will continue.
2) Abortion will run rampant.
3) Teenagers will be out of control.
4) Fewer people will fear God.
5) Fewer people will submit to authority.
6) The general mind-set will be to do it if it feels good.
7) Power within the church will diminish.
8) Segregation and hatred within the church will continue.
9) Man will be feared, rather than God.
10) Prayer and discipline will be taken out of schools.
11) Drug overdoses will continue.

12) Schools will turn into war zones.

Do we really want to stay on this path? Allowing this to happen while we sleep in sin is not good. Let me ask you this: Is God pleased with your actions? Are you paving the way the Word of God wants you to go? Or are you allowing the world to choose your path?

The only true path to the Father is to awaken from your enchanted sleep in Sin Forest. It won't be easy to escape, because the enemy will put up a fight to keep you there. Revelation 12:9 says, "And the great dragon was thrown down, that ancient serpent, who is called the devil and satan, the deceiver of the Whole World. He was thrown down to the earth, and his angels were thrown down with him." That is why we wrestle not against flesh and blood.

You're probably wondering why God didn't throw that joker to another planet. I wish God had banished the devil from earth, so that he couldn't tempt or trick you into thinking that there are many ways to the Father. If God had put the devil on another planet, would we be content in Christ Jesus? Would we praise the Father through all eternity? Don't forget, however, that the flesh cannot be made perfect and should remain on the cross. James 3:2 says, "For we all stumble in many ways. And if anyone does not stumble in what he says, he is a perfect man, able also to bridle his whole body." Romans 13:14 says, "But put on the Lord Jesus Christ, and make no provision for the flesh, to gratify its desires."

If you want to put on the Lord Jesus Christ, you have to experience a great awakening and come out of the enchantment sleep in Sin Forest. Do not become complacent, church, because it's high time to wake up. If you refuse to awaken, you will start to worship strange and unknown gods. Why open up that can of worms?

TWO

Worshipping Strange and Unknown Gods

It's time for the church to get out of the enchantment sleep in Sin Forest, because you need to be careful who or what you are worshipping, especially today. If you are not worshipping and serving the true living God, then you are worshipping unknown gods. The Israelites have always been God's chosen people, but when Moses went up Mount Sinai to get the Ten Commandments from God, the Israelites got bored and made strange gods. "And he received the gold from their hand and fashioned it with a graving tool and made a golden calf" (Exodus 32:4 KJV). So God told Moses to go back down to the Israelites:

> And the Lord said to Moses, "Go down, for your people, whom you brought up out of the land of Egypt, have corrupted themselves. They have turned aside quickly out of the way that I commanded them. They have made for themselves a golden calf and have worshiped it and sacrificed to it and said, 'These are your gods, O Israel, who brought you up out of the land of Egypt!'" And the Lord said to Moses, "I have seen this people, and behold, it is a stiff-necked people." (Exodus 32:7–9 KJV)

It was easy for God to take the Israelites out of Egypt, but it was difficult for the Israelites to separate themselves from the pagan gods of Egypt because they were trapped in the enchantment sleep in Sin Forest.

God was getting ready to consume the Israelites, and His wrath would have come upon them swiftly and mightily, but He relented when Moses intervened. Moses didn't know that down the road, those same people would make him so angry that he disobeyed God. The people for whom you stand in the gap will probably be the same people to prevent you from entering your own Promised Land. When people provoke you, your anger will cloud your mind and cause you to do something that you will regret.

What golden calf are you conjuring up today? If God doesn't have your whole heart, then you need to examine yourself. God is a jealous God and He will not share you. "The Lord is a jealous and avenging God; the Lord is avenging and wrathful; the Lord takes vengeance on his adversaries and keeps wrath for his enemies" (Nahum 1:2 ESV). "For the Lord your God is a consuming fire, a jealous God" (Deuteronomy 4:24 ESV). Have you allowed sexual immorality, pornography, drugs, alcohol, hatred, envy, unforgiveness, or money to become your golden calf? God is imploring you not to set your mind on evil things:

> So Paul, standing in the midst of the Areopagus, said: "Men of Athens, I perceive that in every way you are very religious. For as I passed along and observed the objects of your worship, I found also an altar with this inscription: 'To the unknown god.' What therefore you worship as unknown, this I proclaim to you. The God who made the world and everything in it, being Lord of heaven and earth, does not live in temples made by man, nor is he served by human hands, as though he needed anything, since he himself gives to all mankind life and breath and everything. And he made from one man every nation of mankind to live on all the face of the earth, having determined allotted periods and the boundaries of their dwelling place, that they should seek God, and perhaps feel their way toward him and find him. Yet he is actually not far from each one of us, for 'In him we live and move and have our being'; as even some of your own poets have said, 'For we are indeed his offspring.'" (Acts 17:22–28 ESV)

What inscription, church, have you written on your heart?

In that time of national decline, despite their promise to keep the covenant (Joshua 24:16–18), the people turned from the Lord and began to worship other gods. "Everyone did what was right in his own eyes" (Joshua 17:6, 21:25). A pattern repeats throughout Joshua: (1) the people abandon the Lord; (2) God punishes them by raising up a foreign power to oppress them; (3) the people cry out to God for deliverance; and (4) God raises up a deliverer, or judge, for them.[6] "If you forsake the Lord and serve foreign gods, then he will turn and do you harm and consume you, after having done you good" (Joshua 24:20 ESV). God will consume you, like He did Aaron's two sons, Nadab and Abihu, if you do not awaken and stop worshipping strange and unknown gods. The reason why you conjure up these gods in your mind is that you lack a healthy fear of God. "Behold, the eye of the Lord is upon them that fear Him, upon them that hope in His mercy" (Psalm 33:18 KJV).

Aaron, the priest, anointed his four sons to be consecrated to minister in the priests' office. "And Nadab and Abihu died before the Lord, when they offered strange fire before the Lord, in the wilderness of Sinai, and they had no children" (Numbers 3:4 KJV). God had forewarned them and given them specific instructions about what to do and the order in which it should be done. "And Nadab and Abihu, the sons of Aaron, took either of them his censer and put fire therein, and put incense thereon, and offered strange fire before the Lord, which he commanded them not. And there went out fire from the Lord, and devoured them, and they died before the Lord" (Leviticus 10:1–2 KJV).

When God tells you not to do something, please take heed. Nadab and Abihu called God's bluff, and they died for it. Obedience to God is better than sacrifice. Nadab and Abihu were guilty of a presumptuous and unwarranted intrusion into a sacred office that did not belong to them. Their unwise, dangerous action was an abomination before the Lord. They knew the oil had to be anointed, so why didn't they take Aaron their censer before putting incense in it? God is a God of order. Church, I implore you to listen and take heed of what the Spirit is saying. God loves you and He doesn't want to consume you, but He is a jealous God. He wants you to worship Him and Him alone.

First Kings describes the construction of the temple in Jerusalem and shows the importance of proper worship. God's faithfulness to His people is shown as He sent prophets, most notably Elijah, to warn them not to serve other gods.

In the third chapter of Daniel, King Nebuchadnezzar erected a golden image, ninety feet tall and nine feet wide, and commanded his people to fall down and worship it. They were warned that when they heard music—the horn, pipe, lyre, trigon, harp, or bagpipe—they should fall down and worship the golden image. If they refused, they would immediately be cast into a fiery furnace.

In Daniel 2:49, Daniel asked the king to appoint Shadrach, Meshach, and Abednego over the affairs of the province of Babylon, while Daniel himself remained at the king's court. The three Hebrew boys had a strong relationship with the one true living God, who sometimes will place people in a difficult situation just to see if they will serve Him and Him alone. The three Hebrew boys refused to fall down and worship Nebuchadnezzar's golden idol, so the Chaldeans reported this to King Nebuchadnezzar.

The king challenged the only true living God by saying to Shadrach, Meshach, and Abednego, "Who is the God who will deliver you out of my hands?" The three boys kept their composure and said, "O Nebuchadnezzar, we have no need to answer you in this matter" (Daniel 3:16 ESV). They told the king that their God was able to deliver them from the fiery furnace. Now that's the kind of strong and powerful faith that the Lord requires of us.

The king was so angry that he ordered the furnace to be heated seven times hotter than usual. Shadrach, Meshach, and Abednego were bound by some of the king's soldiers and cast into the fiery furnace, where the fire was so hot that it killed the soldiers themselves. The king was astounded when he observed not three but four men walking in the midst of the fire loosed and unbound. King Nebuchadnezzar said, "The form of the fourth is like the Son of God." Jesus was in the midst of the fiery furnace with Shadrach, Meshach, and Abednego, and the fire had no power over them. Their hair wasn't singed nor were their coats damaged; they didn't even smell of fire.

Because of the strong faith of Shadrach, Meshach, and Abednego, the king made a new decree: "Any people, nation, or language that speaks anything against the God of Shadrach, Meshach, and Abednego shall be torn limb from limb, and their houses laid in ruins, for there is no other god who is able to rescue in this way" (Daniel 3:29 ESV). Church, no other god can save and deliver like our God.

If you don't have a strong faith, then pray to God and He will give it to you. After the three Hebrew boys stood up for God, he promoted them. The God that you serve will promote you, too, after you have gone through your own fiery furnace, whatever that might be for you. You might ask, "Why is God not showing Himself mighty today?" Well, that's a great question. Perhaps because of our lack of faith, or maybe because we don't fear Him as we should. Stories like this one from the book of Daniel are supposed to increase your faith in Him. It's okay to tell God that you believe, but that you also need help with your unbelief. God can work with that, if you let Him.

It's time to wake up, oh mighty men and women of God, and return to worshipping the one and only true living God. If you run back to your first love and truly worship Him, your ignorance and sleeping in sin should cease. We need to reinscribe on our hearts, "As for me and my house, we will serve only the Lord." The God that made the heavens and earth is the only one I want to worship.

If you do not want to worship strange and unknown gods any longer, then take heed of 1 Peter 5:8 and practice sober vigilance. Why? Because your adversary, the devil, walks about like a roaring lion, seeking whom he may devour. While you are physically sleeping, your warring angel is on assignment and watching over you. But if you are sleepwalking in sin every day, then you are not obeying the scripture where God tells you to be alert and watchful. The Bible compares the devil to a lion, and lions sneak up on their prey, who don't even realize that the lion is there until it's too late. When a lion's prey is at its most vulnerable state—isolated or injured, for example—that's when the lion will pounce. "Does a lion roar in the forest, when he has no prey? Does a young lion cry out from his den, if he has taken nothing?" (Amos 3:4 KJV).

That is exactly what the devil is doing to people who are in the enchantment sleep in Sin Forest. You don't realize that the devil is sneaking up on you, because you have allowed the sleep in sin to isolate you. When you're sleeping in sin, you think you can walk this Christian life alone.

satan is determined to isolate you from other Christians, and he'll tell you that there is no way to escape your sin and that your fellow Christians will judge you. The devil will tell you that everyone else is getting away with sin, so why shouldn't you?

Awaken from the lies of the enemy, and realize that there is strength in numbers. The devil wants to keep the church to stay divided, with each of us on our own little church island. The Bible says, "Can two walk together, except they be agreed?" (Amos 3:3 KJV). We need to get it together on earth among our Christian brothers and sisters, because God isn't going to force that on us.

Why doesn't God want us to worship strange gods? Not only because He is a jealous God, but also because we need to know who we are in Christ Jesus. "But ye are a chosen generation, a royal priesthood, an holy nation, a peculiar people; that ye should shew forth the praises of him who hath called you out of darkness into his marvelous light: Which in time past were not a people, but are now the people of God: which had not obtained mercy, but now have obtained mercy" (1 Peter 2:9–10 KJV). Why do you want to walk in agreement with the devil? When you keep listening to his lies, you are agreeing with what he's telling you.

Mandy Hall said, "Sometimes it takes heartbreak to shake us awake and help us see we are worth so much more than we're settling for." Does it really have to take heartbreak to wake us up? Can we not see that we are valuable and precious to God? That's why He sent His son to die for us, but do not defer your own salvation by not knowing Him. "Hope deferred makes the heart sick, but a desire fulfilled is a tree of life" (Proverbs 13:12 ESV).

The church has been lulled into a deep sleep in sin by the enemy and doesn't know how to escape. That's how cunning the devil is—he'll gradually introduce you to something without you realizing that he's behind it. We think that it's okay to worship all these strange and unknown gods, because this deep sleep in sin has paralyzed us. The church has been lulled into a stupor of fatigue, such that our passivity is reminiscent of the television series *The Walking Dead*. The enemy has deceptively robbed us of our confidence and self-reliance.

Has the church really lost its influence? Are we just silently going through the motions, or do we still have a voice? Our silence implies that we're in agreement with whomever is speaking. Napoleon said, "Ten people who speak make more noise than ten thousand who are silent."[7] The church was quiet after the Roe v. Wade ruling, and when one person spoke up against prayer in our schools, and when drugs such as marijuana were legalized. Instead, the church should be trusting Jesus Christ to order our footsteps. If you want to be blessed, just start trusting God, the lover of your soul. Psalm 119:105 says, "Your word is a lamp to my feet and a light to my path."

The church should be gentle like a dove but bold as a lion. What does this mean? It means that we need to boldly and confidently speak what the Lord is saying to the church in love. We can be neither judgmental nor quiet any longer. Isaiah 62:1 says, "For Zion's sake I will not keep silent, and for Jerusalem's sake I will not be quiet, until her righteousness goes forth as brightness, and her salvation as a burning torch." So church, for the sake of the unborn children, for the sake of our children in the schools, and for the sake of this land, we must not remain quiet and under the sleep in sin spell of the enemy any longer. We need to snap out of it and tell that old devil that enough is enough. After all, those three Hebrew boys didn't remain silent.

Worshipping strange and unknown gods will cause you to remain silent. The church has adopted the mind-set that all we have to do is just wait on God to take care of things, but God is telling us to speak up and do what He has commanded. I am so happy that my God is a God of action. If God had said, "Well, I'm going to wait and see if they can fix this sin problem by themselves. I'm not sending My only Son to die a horrific death just to fix what they've messed up," then we would have been lost forever. But that's exactly what's happening when we refuse to do anything about what's going on in our country today.

Jesus said, "Truly, truly, I say to you, whoever believes in me will also do the works that I do; and greater works than these will he do, because I am going to the Father" (John 14:12). Jesus gave us the Holy Spirit, which is all we need to do greater work than He did. When Jesus walked on this earth, He didn't remain quiet. He spoke into people's lives and healed them. He set the captives free. He overturned the moneychangers' tables when they disrespected the temple. Jesus didn't say, "Well, they're just having fun. It's okay." So why is the church so quiet today?

The church remained quiet during slavery and while African Americans were being lynched. The church remained quiet during Roe v. Wade. Now the church is still quiet. We see things going on that we know that God is not pleased with, but we refuse to say anything. Whom does the church fear—man or God? When we are silent, it's because we fear man. But if we attack the problem of sin with boldness and confidence, then we are pleasing God.

If we continue to remain quiet, as Lamentation 5:2 warns, "Our inheritance [will be] turned over to strangers, our homes to foreigners." God has blessed this land tremendously. So do we really want to stay under the devil's sleep-in-sin trance and allow this situation to continue, or are we going to speak up in the name of Jesus? Lamentation 5:21 says, "Restore us to yourself, O Lord, that we may be restored! Renew our days as of old." I want our children to be safe at school and our unborn children to be safe in their mothers' wombs. Second Chronicles 7:14 says, "If my people who are called by My name humble themselves, and pray and seek My face and turn from their wicked ways, then I will hear from heaven and will forgive their sin and heal their land." Church, we need a great awakening so that our land can be healed. We cannot stay under the devil's sleep-in-sin spell any longer.

Why are we having a problem trusting God? Psalm 62:8 says, "Trust in Him at all times, O people; pour out your hearts to Him, for God is our refuge." The church needs to rely totally on Jesus in the midst of adversity and turn our backs on those strange and unknown gods. We need to consistently trust Jesus with every fiber of our souls, so that we can once again flourish in His presence.

Psalm 40:4 says, "Blessed is the man who makes the Lord his trust, who does not look to the proud, to those who turn aside to false gods." Church, it's time to wake up and put away those false gods. How do we know we've been lulled into a deep sleep? Because we're more concerned about what people think of the church than about what God thinks. We're working hard to get man's approval instead of God's approval. The church is supposed to pave the way, but instead we allow the world to dictate what is and isn't acceptable. It's time for the church to wake up.

God is our refuge and strength, an ever-present help in times of trouble. When we trust God, we don't need to be concerned with cataclysmic events such as natural disasters, terrorism, serial killers, or environmental catastrophes.

Why did the church allow prayer and discipline to be taken out of the schools? Because we think it's okay to let people worship strange and unknown gods. So now kids run rampant and act disrespectfully toward their teachers and other authority figures, people carry guns into schools, and child-on-child crime is out of control. We let our kids play addictive video games that desensitize them to violent graphics that are far too realistic. Teenagers who have played violent video games since the age of four no longer know what's real and what isn't. Is this how you want to raise your kids? You are allowing your children to worship strange and unknown gods in the form of a video game, unless they accept Jesus as their Lord and Savior and the Holy Spirit quickens them.

Church, the time for being lethargic is over. Psalm 51:10 says, "Create in me a clean heart, O God, and renew a right spirit within me." He will do it if you just ask and accept Jesus as your Lord and Savior. God wants to renew His Spirit within your children. He doesn't want the devil to control them. Parents, if you don't listen to anything else that I say, please heed this! If you love your children, stop letting them play violent video games, or at least ensure that the blood-and-guts graphics are turned off. Proverbs 12:15 says, "The way of a fool is right in his own eyes, but a wise man listens to advice." Proverbs 22:6 says, "Train up a child in the way he should go; even when he is old he will not depart from it." Stop allowing violent video games and television violence to program the minds of your children. A child doesn't know any better, but you do.

If the church experiences a great awakening, we will marvel at the beauty of a life intertwined with God's presence rather than worshipping strange and unknown gods. The church should be rejoicing as we journey together in intimate communion with Him and enjoy the adventure of finding ourselves by losing ourselves in Him. Second Corinthians 5:17 says, "Therefore, if anyone is in Christ, he is a new creation. The old has passed away; behold, the new has come." We are no longer under the sleep-in-sin spell of the devil. God wants to jolt us out of that deep pit and defibrillate us to wake us up. John 15:4 says, "Abide in Me, and I in you. As the branch cannot bear fruit by itself, unless it abides in the vine, neither can you, unless you abide in me." God wants us to remain in Him so that He can remain in us.

To stay connected to the vine, our life source, we must wake up. That's the only way we can bear fruit and be effective for this generation. Our omniscient God is not surprised at what's going on in the world today, but He created us so that we can make a difference. If we want to become the people God created us to be, we must walk closer to Him. Then we'll grow and flourish as He opens our eyes to see more of His presence and the glory that is all around us. I want to see more of His glory each and every day.

Don't you know that God is always speaking to His children? His sheep know His voice when they hear it, but if you are under the devil's sleep-in-sin trance, you won't be able to hear it. So wake up and listen to what the Spirit of the Lord is saying. It is past time for God's children to run back to their first love. This should be our highest priority. When we journey through life in His presence, His glory illuminates the world around us. Isaiah 50:4 says, "The sovereign Lord has given me an instructed tongue, to know the word that sustains the weary." He wakens me morning by morning and opens my ears to hear his teachings.

Revelation 2:4 says, "Yet I hold this against you. You have forsaken your first love." Church, it's high time to stop worshipping those strange and unknown gods. Let's hurry back to our first love and be awakened in Jesus's name. If the church does not awaken, it will have no reverent fear of God and continue to serve strange and unknown gods.

~ THREE ~

No Reverence Fear of God

How do we know if we are in a deep sleep in sin? If we do not have any reverent fear of God. We fear God by asking for wisdom: "The fear of the Lord is the beginning of wisdom" (Psalm 111:10). We fear God by walking in the light of Jesus, and we reverence Him by recognizing who He is. This kind of fear is healthy for us.

Unfortunately we fear man more than we fear God. We care about what other people say and think about us, rather than how God feels and thinks about us. We try to please man and not God. When we do these things, we are walking in fear. Every time we turn on the news, we hear about suicide bombers, terrorist attacks, and active shooters in our schools. The enemy has made us so afraid that we are afraid to live a victorious life, but God tells us not to fear other gods. "With whom the Lord had made a covenant, and charged them, saying, Ye shall not fear other gods, nor bow yourselves to them, nor serve them, nor sacrifice to them" (2 Kings 17:35 KJV). As discussed in the previous chapter, when we worship strange and unknown gods, we fear them instead of the Almighty God. We wrestle not against flesh and blood, but against the devil and his demons. So why should we fear those gods? Our God is greater and stronger, because He is omnipotent.

We are supposed to serve the Lord with reverent fear. "Serve the Lord with fear, and rejoice with trembling" (Psalm 2:11 KJV). We are supposed to be walking in wisdom, not sleeping in sin. "The fear of the Lord is the beginning of knowledge: but fools despise wisdom and instruction" (Proverbs 1:7 KJV). "For as the heaven is high above the earth, so great is his mercy toward them that fear him" (Psalm 103:11 KJV). First John 4:18 says, "There is no fear in love, but perfect love casts out fear. For fear has to do with punishment, and whoever fears has not been perfected in love." We will not be perfected in love if we continue to live in the sleep in sin dungeon. But if we are walking in love, then we are living a victorious life free of fear, because fear is a liar.

Second Timothy 1:7 says, "For God gave us a spirit not of fear but of power and love and self-control." But how can we walk in His power, love, and self-control when we are asleep in Sin Dungeon? We will live in fear if we remain in the devil's sleep in Sin Dungeon, but if we awaken, then we can say with confidence, "The Lord is my helper; I will not fear; what can man do to me?" (Hebrews 13:6 ESV). "The Lord is on my side; I will not fear. What can man do to me?" (Psalm 118:6 ESV).

Matthew 26:41 says, "Watch and pray that you may not enter into temptation. The Spirit indeed is willing, but the flesh is weak." The church is not watching and praying. We are sleeping in sin. The church has caused temptation to creep in, because we are walking in the flesh and opening the door for the devil to enter. When temptation knocks at our door, we should not answer it. When we sleep in sin, we allow temptation to take control of our lives. That's not God-fearing wisdom. God wants us to submit to Him—not to the devil and his temptations.

How do we know if we are yielding to the devil? Is it when we open the door to pleasing the flesh? When we set our minds on fleshly desires, we are submitting to the devil. We should know what our temptations are by now. Mine are pornography, lust of the flesh, lust of the eyes, and pride of life. Your temptation might be drugs, alcohol, greed, gossiping, sexual immorality, lasciviousness, and so on. These things are spirits that come from the devil, but that is not who we are in Christ Jesus. The devil will continue to throw these fiery darts at us if we do not awaken.

James 4:7 says, "Therefore submit to God, resist the devil and he will flee." It's imperative that we submit to God rather than to the devil. God created us in His image and sent His Son to die on the cross for our sin. God is the alpha and omega, the first and last, the beginning and end. God tells us that we are the apple of His eye. It's sad that when God's people continue to sleepwalk in sin through the day, they'll eventually bump into

21

an obstacle until it annihilates them. (Read 2 Corinthians 4:16–18 and 1 Corinthians 15:20–23.)

God's people are preoccupied with our pasts, our plans for the future, and decisions we need to make in the present. Our pasts tend to torment us until condemnation sets in like gangrene or cancer. Those of us who are caught up in our futures tend to worry about what's on the road ahead; what would we do if disease attacked our bodies, for example? Matthew 6:27 says, "Can any of you add a single cubit to his height by worrying?" We don't realize that we are making these things bigger than God. We are putting our pasts and futures ahead of God.

God tells us not to worry about such things. Matthews 12:29 says, "And do not seek what you are to eat and what you are to drink, nor be worried." God tells us to give our cares to Him: "Casting all your anxieties on him, because he cares for you" (1 Peter 5:7). We need to stop being preoccupied with our pasts, which we cannot change anyway, and stop worrying about our futures, because doing so blinds us to the decisions we need to make today. Jesus died for our past, present, and future sins. The church needs to stop listening to the lying voice of the devil and just see him as a noisemaker.

We must cast our cares upon Jesus, rather than habitually responding to the voice of the enemy without even being aware of it. When God's people choose to live this way, we will find a dullness creeping into our lives. We will continue to sleepwalk in sin throughout our days, following well-worn, routine paths.

But thanks be to God, the creator of the universe, for He will not allow us to stay in that state of mind. He will not leave us circling in our rutted paths, but He will lead us along fresh trails of adventure, revealing to us things that we didn't know and can't comprehend. Psalm 32:8 says, "I will instruct you and teach you in the way you should go; I will counsel you with my eye upon you." For God to instruct and teach us in the way we should go, we have to wake up from the sleep in sin.

That is one reason why it's so vital to stay in complete communication with God, allowing the Holy Spirit to direct our paths. "Your word is a lamp to my feet and a light to my path" (Psalm 119:105 ESV). God's Word instructs us at every step of the way, but we must be awakened to follow His Word. Remember that God has clothed us in His righteousness and holiness. (Read Isaiah 61:10 and Ephesians 1:7–8 on the forgiveness of sins.)

God said that He will not put any more on us than we can bear. But if we choose to stay in the enchantment sleep in Sin Forest, the enemy will definitely put more on us than we can bear. Suppose a boat has an anchor on a short rope that allows the boat to drift slightly before the taut line tugs it back toward the center. Likewise, when you and I start to drift away from God, His Holy Spirit within us gives us a tug, prompting us to return to Him. Hebrew 6:19 says, "We have this as a sure and steadfast anchor of the soul, a hope that enters into the inner place behind the curtain." Our souls should be anchored in the Lord. Secret sins that we hide from God can split off and develop lives of their own, controlling us even when we don't realize it. (Read Psalm 139:1–4, 23–24 and 1 John 4:18.) The sins that we continue to hide will become a great wickedness and make it difficult to awaken.

FOUR

Great Wickedness

Isaiah 60:2 says, "For behold, darkness shall cover the earth and thick darkness the peoples; but the Lord will arise upon you and His glory will be seen upon you." That's how it was in the days of Sodom and Gomorrah. Genesis 13:13 says, "Now the men of Sodom were wicked and sinners against Jehovah exceedingly." Their thoughts were consumed by wickedness. Genesis 13:10 says, "And Lot lifted up his eyes, and beheld all the plain of the Jordan, that it was well watered everywhere, before Jehovah destroyed Sodom and Gomorrah, like the garden of Jehovah, like the land of Egypt as thou goest unto Zoar."

Lot chose to reside in Sodom because the land was beautiful. He refused to see Sodom as being wicked, and he didn't speak up and tell the people of Sodom that their lives were an abomination before God. God was not pleased with Sodom, where homosexuality, orgies, and pornography were running rampant and people's thoughts were consumed by wickedness. Has America become like Sodom and Gomorrah? Will our thoughts be consumed by wickedness and greed? Will the church remain in the sleep in sin, causing the wrath of God to fall on our land?

The church must not remain silent, as Lot did, when it comes to great wickedness and thick darkness. The church needs to experience a great awakening and say, "Enough is enough!" before it's too late. The church needs to take a stand and let America know that God loves us, but He hates our sin.

Sin had become great in the land of Sodom and Gomorrah. Two angels, appearing as men, went into the city to Lot's house. Genesis 19:5

tells us that the men of Sodom "called unto Lot, and said unto him, where are those men that came in to your house this night? Bring them out unto us, that we may know them." The men of Sodom didn't know that the two strangers were angels, but they were so wicked that they probably wouldn't have cared anyway.

The church needs to put a guard around its heart and start thinking about things that are pure, true, and lovely. "Finally, brothers, whatever is true, whatever is honorable, whatever is just, whatever is pure, whatever is lovely, whatever is commendable, if there is any excellence, if there is anything worthy of praise, think about these things" (Philippians 4:8 ESV).

Gomorrah symbolizes wickedness, idolatry, immorality, pride, and prosperity. Ezekiel 16:49 says, "Behold, this was the iniquity of thy sister Sodom: pride, fullness of bread, and prosperous ease was in her and in her daughters; neither did she strengthen the hand of the poor and needy." God is speaking to us. Is America on the same path as Sodom and Gomorrah? They were beautiful, prosperous cities, but they were full of pride—just like America. Instead of strengthening the hand of the poor and needy, we are weakening the hand of the poor by giving everything to the rich—just like Sodom and Gomorrah. I believe that Sodom and Gomorrah had a religious spirit, but that the church kept silent while great wickedness took control. We need to heed God's warnings. When He tries to get our attention, we need to have a great awakening and listen. (Read 2 Peter 2:1–22.)

The church has been lulled to sleep by the devil in Sin Dungeon, and we have turned to our vomit again like pigs wallowing in the mire. As gross and ludicrous as this sounds, God painted this analogy for us as a sign for us to wake up. Jude 7 says, "Just as Sodom and Gomorrah and the surrounding cities, which likewise indulged in sexual immorality and pursued unnatural desire, serve as an example by undergoing a punishment of eternal fire." They gave themselves over to fornication and went after strange flesh, and their example should cause us to awaken so that we won't suffer the punishment of eternal fire. Do not turn the grace of God into lasciviousness and deny our only Lord and Master, Jesus Christ, by remaining in the sleep in Sin Dungeon. Jude 4 says, "For certain people have crept in unnoticed who long ago were designated for this condemnation, ungodly people, who pervert the grace of our God into sensuality and deny our Master and Lord, Jesus Christ." It was ludicrous for them to do such a thing.

Church, if we refuse to awaken, then we will fall for this same lifestyle. Is America headed down the path of perverting the grace of our God into sensuality? Are we getting to the point of denying our Lord and Savior, Jesus Christ? Isaiah 3:9 says, "They declare their sin as Sodom, they hide it not." We have become callous and convinced ourselves that this is the norm. Woe unto us! In America, we don't hide our sin because we aren't ashamed of it. We have become like Sodom and Gomorrah. Do we really want the judgment of God to come upon us?

Sodom symbolizes immorality and vileness, but I refuse to believe the same of America. This is not how God wants us to live. He wants us to have lives that are pleasing in His sight—lives full of abundance in which our souls prosper. God does not want us to live in bondage ever again.

Malachi 4:1 tells us that a day is coming, burning like a furnace, when all the proud, all who work wickedness, shall be as stubble, to be put into a furnace and burned up. I'm looking forward to that day. I'm looking forward to the day where this newfangled thing called wickedness will burn as a furnace. People who are wicked and prideful will have a lobotomy performed on them by the Holy Spirit, and then they will no longer practice such wickedness.

Hallelujah! I'm praying that a day will come when God's people will experience a great awakening from the devil sleep in sin. When God's people wake up, we can change our world by being strong in the Lord and relying on His power. When we put on the whole armor of God, we are putting on the Lord Jesus Christ. "But put on the Lord Jesus Christ, and make no provision for the flesh, to gratify its desires" (Romans 13:14 ESV).

> Put on the whole armor of God, that you may be able to stand against the schemes of the devil. For we do not wrestle against flesh and blood, but against the rulers, against the authorities, against the cosmic powers over this present darkness, against the spiritual forces of evil in the heavenly places. Therefore take up the whole armor of God, that you may be able to withstand in the evil day, and having done all, to stand firm. Stand therefore,

having fastened on the belt of truth, and having put on the breastplate of righteousness, and, as shoes for your feet, having put on the readiness given by the gospel of peace. In all circumstances take up the shield of faith, with which you can extinguish all the flaming darts of the evil one; and take the helmet of salvation, and the sword of the Spirit, which is the word of God, praying at all times in the Spirit, with all prayer and supplication. To that end, keep alert with all perseverance, making supplication for all the saints. (Ephesians 6:10–18 ESV)

The battle is not ours, it's the Lord's. We do not wrestle against flesh and blood, and we have an enemy in the spirit realm who doesn't want us to put on our armor correctly. The devil wants us to remain in the sleep in sin so he can continue to control us. If the church really gets a revelation of who we are in Christ Jesus, we can be unstoppable. We can be bold as a lion but gentle as a dove. Each piece of our armor has to be sealed and activated by the Holy Spirit. We will be covered from the crowns of our heads to the soles of our feet and walking by faith and not in fear. The purpose for putting on the whole armor is to protect us from the devil's fiery darts—fear, worrying, sexual immorality, addictions, fornication, and perversion. In a nutshell, they are the lust of the flesh, lust of the eyes, and pride of life.

The first piece of armor is the belt of truth. How do we know that we are wearing the belt of truth? When we confess that Jesus is the way, the truth, and the life. "Jesus said to him, 'I am the way, the truth, and the life. No one comes to the Father except through Me'" (John 14:6 NKJV). Truth is knowing who we are in Christ Jesus and that Jesus is the light. The truth is that we can do all things through Christ Jesus, if we are empowered by the Holy Spirit. "God is Spirit, and those who worship Him must worship in spirit and truth" (John 4:24 NKJV). "For you were once darkness, but now you are light in the Lord. Walk as children of light [for the fruit of the Spirit is in all goodness, righteousness, and truth]" (Ephesians 5:8–9 NKJV). Truth knows that when we activate the belt of truth and seal it with the Holy Spirit, the devil is a defeated foe.

The truth is that we need the trinity in our lives every day. God is the manager who gives Jesus an assignment and ensures that it will get done. Jesus is the doer of the assignment, the worker bee, through the Crucifixion, the conquering of death, and the Resurrection. The Holy Spirit checks off the work that Jesus completed and puts His seal of approval on it. Now we just have to ensure that the belt of truth has been sealed and activated by the Holy Spirit. Isaiah 11:5 says, "Righteousness shall be the belt of his waist, and faithfulness the belt of his loins."

Our second piece of armor is the breastplate of righteousness, which protects our hearts and upper torsos. We have to be in good standing with God, believing and trusting Him like Abraham did in Genesis 15:6. When Abraham believed God, it was counted to him as righteousness. Let it be counted to us as righteous before the Lord that we believe in God and that His Word is true. The Lord will reward us for our righteousness and faithfulness. (Read 1 Samuel 26:23.) Notice that the belt and breastplate are sealed together by righteousness and faithfulness. The Lord will lead us in His righteousness. (Read Psalm 5:8.) We need to put on righteousness and it will clothe us. (Read Job 29:14.)

The church needs to walk in the way of righteousness. (Read Proverbs 8:20.) The church must fulfill all righteousness. (Read Matthew 3:15.) The church must have a hunger and a thirst for righteousness to be considered blessed. (Read Matthew 5:6.) The church must serve Him without fear, but in holiness and righteousness all our days. (Read Luke 1:74–75.) The church shall live by faith to be considered righteous. (Read Romans 1:17 and 2 Corinthians 5:21.) The church has to be training in righteousness by studying and meditating on the Word of God. (Read 2 Timothy 3:15.) After we have been trained in righteousness, we must practice it. (Read 1 John 2:29 and 3:7.)

With the third piece of our armor, our feet are shod in preparation for the gospel of peace. The peace referred to here is called "Shalom" of God. The church should be seeking peace. (Read Psalm 34:14 and 1 Peter 3:11.) If the church is walking with God, He will make our enemies be at peace with us. (Read Proverbs 16:7.) If we keep our minds stayed on Him, He will keep us in perfect peace. (Read Isaiah 26:3 and Romans 8:6.) God will make a covenant of peace with us. (Read Ezekiel 34:25.) We should be walking with Jesus, the Prince of Peace, because He is our peace. (Read

Ephesians 2:14.) The Bible tells us that God is not a God of confusion but of peace, so the church should be a church of peace. (Read 1 Corinthians 14:33.) One of the fruits of the Spirit is peace, so we should be eating peace. (Read Galatians 5:22.) The church should be preaching peace and making peace. (Read Ephesians 2:17, Colossians 1:20, and Colossians 3:15.) If we are preaching and walking in peace, it will be multiplied to us. (Read 2 Peter 1:2 and Jude 1:2.) Then the peace of God will guard our hearts and minds through Christ Jesus. "And the peace of God, which surpasses all understanding, will guard your hearts and your minds in Christ Jesus" (Philippians 4:7 ESV). We need to renew our spiritual vitality by pursuing peace in Jesus's name.

The fourth piece of armor that we need to put on, regardless of the circumstances we're experiencing, is the shield of faith. The primary purpose of the shield of faith is to extinguish the flaming darts that the devil fires at us. No matter what situation we're facing, we need to ensure that our shield of faith is sealed with the Holy Spirit so that the enemy's fiery darts will bounce off like water on a duck's back. All we need is the faith of a mustard seed. (Read Luke 17:6.) Faith comes by hearing the Word of God. (Read Romans 10:17.) The church is justified by faith in Christ. (Read Galatians 2:16.)

Our fifth piece of armor is the helmet of salvation. If we are not saved, the other pieces of armor won't work. If you do not know Jesus Christ as your Lord and Savior, then now is the time to do so. You can just say a simple prayer:

> Jesus, I believe you are the Son of God and born of a virgin. I believe you died on an old rugged cross for my past, present, and future sin. I believe you rose from the dead on the third day with all Resurrection power. I believe you sealed everything through the Holy Spirit. I believe in the Trinity—God the Father, the Son, and the Holy Spirit—and that they are one. Now I ask you to forgive me of my sin and come into my heart so that I can have a personal relationship with You. In Jesus's name, amen!

The final piece of the armor that we need to pick up is the sword of the Spirit, which is the Word of God—praying at all times in the Spirit, with all prayer and supplication. The church has to pray the Word of God without ceasing in the Spirit. "For the word of God is living and active, sharper than any two-edged sword, piercing to the division of soul and of spirit, of joints and of marrow, and discerning the thoughts and intentions of the heart" (Hebrews 4:12 ESV).

When we put on all the pieces of armor and they are sealed and activated by the Holy Spirit, we become the living Word of God, a walking Bible. So wherever we go, we must speak life and not death. The devil doesn't want you to experience a great awakening, because if you get a revelation of who you really are, the gates of hell shall not prevail against you. (Read Matthew 16:18.) The church is supposed to open its mouth with boldness and make known the mystery of the gospel. John 1:14 says, "And the Word was made flesh, and dwelt among us, and we beheld his glory, the glory as of the only begotten of the Father, full of grace and truth." So when we put on Jesus Christ, we are putting on the Word. Romans 13:14 says, "But put on the Lord Jesus Christ, and make no provision for the flesh, to gratify its desires." We are putting on the Word of God when we put on the Lord Jesus Christ. When the church finally experiences a great awakening, we will be walking in wisdom. (Read Ephesians 5:15–16.)

~ FIVE ~

Practicing Unrighteousness

How do you know if you are sleeping in sin? When you are blatantly practicing unrighteousness, you are practicing lawlessness:

> Everyone who makes a practice of sinning also practices lawlessness; sin is lawlessness. You know that he appeared in order to take away sins, and in him there is no sin. No one who abides in him keeps on sinning; no one who keeps on sinning has either seen him or known him. Little children, let no one deceive you. Whoever practices righteousness is righteous, as he is righteous. Whoever makes a practice of sinning is of the devil, for the devil has been sinning from the beginning. The reason the Son of God appeared was to destroy the works of the devil. No one born of God makes a practice of sinning, for God's seed abides in him; and he cannot keep on sinning, because he has been born of God. This is evident, that who are the children of God, and who are the children of the devil: whoever does not practice righteousness is not of God, nor is the one who does not love his brother. (1 John 3:4–10 ESV)

If you wake up in the morning and tell yourself, "I'm going to practice sinning today. I'm going out to please the flesh," then you are walking in the sleep in sin. I cannot even fathom how someone can premeditate sinning. If you are doing this, then the devil has a strong hold on you. It's beyond me how someone can take another person's life. In the next chapter, I'll talk about walking in unforgiveness and how it can destroy you. God doesn't want you to practice unrighteousness. He wants you to practice righteousness so that you can be righteous before Him. You cannot sit at the same table with righteousness and unrighteousness, because they are contrary to each other. God is righteous and the devil is unrighteous. If you are practicing unrighteousness, then you're a child of the devil and practicing darkness. "Take no part in the unfruitful works of darkness, but instead expose them" (Ephesians 5:11 ESV). God's Word says that it is shameful to speak of those things that you do in secret. The church should not be participating in those things at all, because you are sleeping in sin. "For it is shameful even to speak of the things that they do in secret" (Ephesians 5:12 ESV). The devil wants you to walk in unrighteousness, so that you'll go with him to hell and be separated from God, your creator. God wants His people to be set apart from all unrighteousness, stop fulfilling those fleshly desires, and awaken in Jesus's name.

Second Corinthians 5:18 says, "All this is from God, who through Christ reconciled us to himself and gave us the ministry of reconciliation;" This agape love is in every aspect of your life. Reconciliation is a commitment. Are you committed to the things of Christ? God is pouring out His grace and mercy upon you, though you've done nothing to deserve them. But He knew this over two thousand years ago, when He sent His only begotten son. Second Corinthians 12:9 says, "My grace is sufficient for you, for My strength is made perfect in weakness."

I will gladly boast of my infirmities, that the power of Christ may rest upon me. God has given each of us weaknesses to keep us on our knees and humble. When a peacock spreads his tail feathers, it's very beautiful. But to keep him humble, God also gave him ugly bird claws. Similarly, our weaknesses are supposed to keep us humble. Don't look at your weaknesses as a stumbling block or worry that someone is going to judge you. Judge not, lest you be judged. So allow that thorn in your flesh to open up, and spread your wings like a peacock to keep running to the cross. Ephesians 3:17 says, "That Christ may dwell in your heart through faith; that you, being rooted and grounded in love." If you truly believe this, then I beseech you to perpetually walk in brotherly love.

You might be familiar with the Johari window model, which lays out exactly what a Christian wants you to see. Feedback is solicited in four areas: known by self, known by others, unknown by self, and unknown by others. Information known by self and others goes in quadrant one, the "open/free area," and information unknown by self or others goes in quadrant four, the "unknown area." In the second quadrant, the "blind area," is information known by others but not by self, and the third quadrant, the "hidden area," is for information known by self but not by others. So the open area contains things that you don't mind revealing, and the blind and hidden areas include your hidden, undisclosed sins. This is the dangerous closet where you keep your skeletons, which you don't want anyone else to see.

The danger is that as long as you keep those things hidden, you cannot be delivered. When satan finishes using you like a puppet, he will kill you. The thief comes to steal, kill, and destroy. The unknown is where you hide the sins that you do behind closed doors, such as pornography, adultery, fornication, drug abuse, or alcohol abuse. You hide these things in your heart because you're ashamed and too afraid to talk to a strong believer about them. You want to be delivered from them, but fear of judgment prevents you from disclosing your problems to others. These sins will defeat and destroy you.

Here is the big-five personality model of Jesus:

1. Extroverted—sociable, friendly, and expressive
2. Emotionally stable—secure, calm, and relaxed
3. Agreeable—courteous, forgiving, tolerant, soft hearted, and trusting
4. Conscientious—dependable, organized, and responsible
5. Open to experience—curious, broad-minded, creative, imaginative, and intelligent

These are characteristics of Christ, and they should be your characteristics as well. Jesus had the creative ability to break away from habit-bound thinking and produce novel, useful ideas. He also possessed self-efficacy, a personal belief in His own competencies and abilities in three primary dimensions: magnitude, strength, and generality. When

Jesus walked on this earth in the form of a man, He knew who He was, and He also knew that He and his Father were one. Jesus said, "If you see Me, you see the Father."

One of the speakers at a recent Martin Luther King Jr. prayer breakfast talked about facing adversity when he went to prison for selling drugs. He did not let his surroundings control him. God strategically placed him in the company of entrepreneurs and CEOs, and because he learned all he could from them while he was in prison, he was later able to become a famous chef. Similarly, we read in the Bible that Joseph did not allow his surroundings to control him. Joseph went to prison for a crime that he didn't commit, after Potiphar's wife lied about him because of her lustful heart.

Though Joseph was a handsome young man, he wasn't vain, and he had a strong relationship with God. When God showed Joseph dreams involving his future, Joseph shared them with his brothers and father. His brothers allowed jealousy to creep into their hearts to the point that they threw Joseph into a pit. Then they decided to sell him into slavery, which is how he ended up in Egypt. Actually it was God's plan all along to send Joseph to Egypt to save His people from a seven-year famine. In Egypt, Joseph became second in command in Potiphar's house, where he had access to everything except Potiphar's wife. The flesh is weak, but the Spirit is strong. If Joseph had been lukewarm or in the sleep-in-sin dungeon, he would have given in to the lustful desires of Potiphar's wife, but Joseph was a true follower of God. As a prime example of how men should live even today, Joseph refused to give in to temptation and sleep with Potiphar's wife. Even at the young age of seventeen, Joseph knew that his body was not his own and that his virginity belonged to God. Joseph was a real man, and real men don't sleep around or commit adultery.

When Joseph was in prison, he didn't murmur and complain. He just continued to minister to people. Don't grow weary of doing well or go to sleep without doing the right thing. Joseph didn't. He just kept pleasing the Lord.

God wants your whole heart. total carte blanche control over your life.

From this day forward, start seeing yourself the way God sees you. Tell yourself that you will no longer allow the devil to lull you in a slumberous dungeon. You will be sober and vigilant and stop listening to that roaring lion without teeth who is the adversary. Choose today not to be devoured by the devil any longer. His roar is worse than his bite, and you are sealed with the blood of Jesus. Tell yourself this:

> I choose this day to run the race that is set before me with endurance and perseverance. I choose to stay in my lane and not deviate from it. I choose not to grow weary of doing good. I choose to keep my eyes on the prize that is set before me, which is Jesus Christ. I choose not to let my mind wonder about things that I cannot control. Father, grant me the serenity to change only the things that You allow me to change. God, I want your thought pattern to be my thought pattern, so that I can see people, things, and circumstances the way that Jesus sees them. I choose not to let unrighteousness control me any longer and I choose to take on the mind of Christ. God, I choose this day to trust You by relinquishing control of my life into Your hands. I choose today to let go and recognize Your sovereignty.

"It is better to trust in the Lord than to put confidence in man. It is better to trust in the Lord than to put confidence in princes" (Psalm 118:8–9 KJV). (Read James 5:8–12, which will help you establish your heart for the coming of the Lord.)

Befriending the World

How do you know if you are not awakening? Being friends with the world will cause you to be at enmity with God. This is an indication that you are still walking in unrighteousness and darkness. How do you know if you have made friends with the world? One indication is that you are focusing on worldly things rather than godly things. "You adulterous people! Do you not know that friendship with the world is enmity with God? Therefore whoever wishes to be a friend of the world makes himself an enemy of God. Or do you suppose it is to no purpose that the Scripture says, 'He yearns jealously over the spirit that he has made to dwell in us'?

But he gives more grace. Therefore it says, 'God opposes the proud but gives grace to the humble'" (James 4:4–6 ESV).

Don't allow pride to become your friend. God resists the proud, but He gives grace to the humble. You are being double-minded when you're preoccupied with selfish things and you think about God only part of the time. The church needs to wake up and submit solely to God. How do you know when you have awakened? When you are obeying James 4:7–8, which says "Submit yourselves therefore to God. Resist the devil, and he will flee from you. Draw nigh to God, and he will draw nigh to you. Cleanse your hands, ye sinners; and purify your hearts, ye double minded." Why would anyone in their right mind want to be an enemy of God? God created you in His image and sent His only Son to die on the cross for your sin. He has prepared a place in heaven for you, if you will just believe.

Church, it's time to stop eaten that forbidden fruit that the devil keeps feeding you. Tell that devil that you will no longer be his puppet on a string. Tell him to get back under your feet, just as Jesus rebuked him two thousand years ago. The church needs to wake up and start obeying the voice of God. Abraham was considered blessed, because he obeyed the Lord and kept His commandments. (Read Genesis 26:5.) Do you know that you are under the blessing of Abraham? Obey God's voice only and not the devil's, and then blessings will chase you down.

How do you know if you are in the devil's slumberous dungeon? If you are not bearing fruit. When a branch falls off a tree, it withers up and dies. (Read John 15:4–7.) Similarly, the enemy wants you to wither up and become ineffective for the Lord. The Bible tells us that if we don't have any life in our branches, we'll be thrown into the fire to be burned up. God wants us to awaken and bear fruit. Stop seeing yourself as a fruitless tree. Instead, see yourself as a fruit-bearing branch and stay connected to the vine.

If you continue to walk in unrighteousness, you will continue to walk in unforgiveness.

∽ SIX ∽

Walking in Unforgiveness

"Mark how God's forgiveness causes us to forgive. God forgives us, though we had no cause to sin against him. We must forgive, as he has forgiven us."[8] The devil, our enemy, wants to paralyze you by instilling in you fear, doubt, unforgiveness, depression, unbelief, worry, and hatred. But Jesus wants to liberate you from the devil's assault on your life, family, ministry, work, finances, home, children, business, body, mind, spirit, and relationships. (Read Galatians 6:7–10.)

Let go of your bitterness and leave it at the foot of the cross. All the school shootings result from anger and bitterness building up inside those kids, which leads to unforgiveness. They are listening to the voice of the enemy. Those kids at one time probably got bullied at school, but schools are not doing anything to prevent bullying. So the kids are getting angrier, and that's when the devil takes control and causes you to retaliate. That's what happened to Peter at Gethsemane—when the Roman soldiers came to arrest Jesus, Peter got angry and cut one of the soldier's ears off. The enemy will cause you to meditate on how to act out the killing and whom to target.

Unforgiveness results from not letting go of your anger and bitterness. Let go of your unforgiveness so that you can help someone else do the same. The children of this generation are crying out for help. They don't know how to let unforgiveness go unless you show them, and how can you show them when you're walking in the sin of unforgiveness?

If someone's words make you angry, that person is controlling you, so don't let that happen. Ask the Holy Spirit to help you understand why those words were spoken to you. Sometimes people speak out because of what they are going through; they might be hurting and just need to vent. You don't know what's going on in a person's life unless they share it with you. The closer you are to a person, the more their words can hurt. That's why God's Word tells us to tame the tongue, to put a bridle on it. Once those words have been spoken, they are in the past—and you cannot change the past, although you can change the present and the future. If I strike you, it will hurt for a moment, but then it's in the past. You shouldn't let people treat you like a doormat, but you do need to learn to walk in forgiveness. Holding on to unforgiveness will put crazy thoughts in your head and eventually lead to destruction.

Why would you allow someone to control you with their words or by bullying you? Remember the old saying, "Sticks and stones will break my bones, but words will never hurt me." Toughen up and keep telling yourself that words will never hurt you. There is one person whose words will never hurt you, and that's Jesus, who died on an old rugged cross for your sins. Jesus will tell you that you are a royal priest, His beloved, blessed and highly favored. "You shall be a crown of beauty in the hand of the Lord, and a royal diadem in the hand of your God" (Isaiah 62:3 ESV). I beseech you to see yourself the way God sees you. Do you not realize that you are royalty in God's eyes?

People have told me that I'm a failure, a nobody, and that I'll never amount to anything. If I allowed those words to control my life, then I *would* be a failure, but I've done the exact opposite. I've showed people that I'm determined to be everything that Jesus has called me to be and that I'm somebody because of Christ Jesus. When I was in college and struggling to finish my degree in electrical engineering, I went to one of my professors for help. He advised me to change my major to engineering technology, which wasn't what I wanted to hear from him. I knew that I was destined to become an electrical engineer, so I refused to accept his words. Instead, I buckled down, persevered, and graduated with an electrical engineering degree. It wasn't easy, but I remembered that God told me to go and get an electrical engineering degree.

When I was in the eleventh grade, the principal of my high school recommended me for a summer program in Tuskegee, Alabama, and a friend and I went through it together. The program provided an introduction to the various types of engineering degrees, and God gave me a strong interest in electrical engineering. So when summer break was over, I talked with my high school counselor about becoming an electrical engineer. I was way behind in math, so I had to take several math classes simultaneously. That process gave me an ulcer, but I got all As.

Why am I telling you this? You can become whatever you want to be, but you have to believe in yourself. Develop a personal relationship with God, and He will make provisions for you. I didn't know how I was going to pay for college, but God orchestrated everything. My dad served in the air force, so I was able to go to college on the Alabama G.I. bill, a scholarship program that helped the children and stepchildren of qualified military veterans pay for college. The program paid for my tuition and books, but not my room and board, so I got a Pell grant to help pay for my dorm room. That was all orchestrated by God, so He gets the honor and glory. If my dad had not been injured while serving in the military, I probably would not have gotten my degree. If I had not been obedient to God at the age of seventeen, I would not have become what He called me to be—an electrical engineer. It would have been easy for me to live a selfish life, but I chose not to. So if you want to go to college, trust God and He will make provision for you. "But my God shall supply all your need according to His riches in glory by Christ Jesus" (Philippians 4:19). Does the Word say *some* of your need? No, it says *all* your need.

Do not grieve the Holy Spirit by holding on to bitterness, wrath, anger, and evil words, which lead to unforgiveness. I implore you to stop sleepwalking and allowing the devil to keep you trapped in the dungeon of unforgiveness. It's like a never-ending cycle in which you experience the bitterness over and over again. Every time you see or hear that person's name, you get angrier. Stop listening to the devil, who comes to kill, steal, and destroy. The devil wants you to lash out in anger, because he knows that will eventually destroy you. You can't see the devil, but he's right there behind the scene, putting those thoughts into your mind. (Read Ephesians 4:26–32.)

When He was on the cross, Jesus asked the Father to forgive the men who had put Him here. They hadn't known what they were doing, Jesus knew, because they were in a deep sleep in sin. We're supposed to be like

Jesus, so I implore you to walk in forgiveness and stop giving the devil a stronghold in your life. Pray this prayer with me:

> Father, I thank you for the words that you have spoken over my life. You said that I will become everything you created me to be. Help me to be in alignment with the words that you have spoken over my life. Help me to see myself the way You see me, and not the way that other people see me. You see me as a winner—not a loser. You see me as a royal priest—not a vagabond. You said that I can do all things through Christ Jesus and that You will supply all my needs. Father, I trust You with my whole life. I choose not to grieve the Holy Spirit any longer. I choose to let You take control of my life every day, so that the oil of gladness and righteousness rest upon me. I choose not to walk in anger and bitterness, which lead to unforgiveness. From this day forward, I choose to walk in forgiveness. In Jesus's name, amen!

Walking in unforgiveness will cause you to perfect your flesh and take it back off the cross.

PART TWO

Perfecting the Flesh

SEVEN

Perfect in the Flesh

How do you know that you are in the sleep in sin? When you do not know you have been bewitched by the devil. "O foolish Galatians, who hath bewitched you, that ye should not obey the truth, before whose eyes Jesus Christ hath been evidently set forth, crucified among you? This only would I learn of you, Received ye the Spirit by the works of the law, or by the hearing of faith? Are ye so foolish? Having begun in the Spirit, are ye now made perfect by the flesh? Have ye suffered so many things in vain? If it be yet in vain" (Galatians 3:1–4 KJV). If you continue to walk in the flesh, you will be bewitched by the devil. He will keep you trapped in the sleep in sin and convince you that your flesh is perfect. The devil will tell you that you do not need a savior.

God does not want you to become trapped again. "Stand fast therefore in the liberty wherewith Christ hath made us free, and be not entangled again with the yoke of bondage" (Galatians 5:1 KJV). But the devil is working overtime because he doesn't want you to be a threat to him and the people he wants to keep in the sleep in sin. God wants you to wake up and walk in the Spirit so that you won't give in to the lust of the flesh or become unclean. Perfecting the flesh will not get you into heaven. God said that no flesh will dwell in His presence. "But when anything is exposed by the light, it becomes visible, for anything that becomes visible is light. Therefore it says, 'Awake, O sleeper, and arise from the dead, and Christ will shine on you.' Look carefully then how you walk, not as unwise but as wise, making the best use of the time, because the days are evil" (Ephesians 5:13–16 ESV). God wants you to awaken and walk in wisdom, because the days are evil.

EIGHT

Called Back Into Uncleanness

How do you know that you have not awakened? Is it when you think that God has called you back into uncleanness rather than into sanctification? I beseech you not to fall back into the devil's trap and return to your own vomit. I accepted Jesus Christ as my personal Lord and Savior at the age of seventeen. I remember having a hunger to know God, but the only Bible I had was the King James Version—and when you're a new babe in Christ, that's not the Bible to have. I tried to read the King James Version, but I couldn't understand the *thee*s and *thou*s. I didn't have anyone to show me how to understand it, but I remember talking to God and asking Him to give me the understanding.

Today there are so many versions of the Bible out there that it's confusing. God is not the author of confusion, but the devil wants you to remain confused. God's Word is your weapon against the devil, and he doesn't want you to use it. The devil wants you to stay in the sleep in sin and uncleanness, instead of waking up and becoming a threat to him. First Thessalonians 4:3–8 says that it's not God's will for you to run back to fornication or uncleanness. God wants you to abstain from fornication and flee from sexual immorality. If you obey His will, then you're protected from the devil's fiery darts, but if you remain in the sleep in sin, you have no protection.

When you fornicate, you tie your soul to a demon, and God does not want you to have communion with such. There are a lot of sexually transmitted diseases out there—I call them demons—and they'll get a strong hold on you and never let you go:

> For this is the will of God, even your sanctification, that ye should abstain from fornication: That every one of you should know how to possess his vessel in sanctification and honour; Not in the lust of concupiscence, even as the Gentiles which know not God: That no man go beyond and defraud his brother in any matter: because that the Lord is the avenger of all such, as we also have forewarned you and testified. For God hath not called us unto uncleanness, but unto holiness. He therefore that despiseth, despiseth not man, but God, who hath also given unto us his holy Spirit. (1 Thessalonians 4:3–8 KJV)

Since God has given you His Holy Spirit, it should be easy to abstain from uncleanness, but you have to walk in the Spirit. If you refuse, you will fulfill the lust of the flesh.

You need to place yourself around strong Christians who are on fire for God. Stay away from lukewarm Christians; they cannot help you, because God is getting ready to spew them out of His mouth. God wants you to be either on fire for Him or cold, but not lukewarm. A lukewarm Christian will remain in their comfort zone, because they are complacent. Today's Pharisees and Sadducees in America are called Lukewarm Christians. They are caught up in the religious aspect of the dos and don'ts without having an intimate relationship with God. They just want to give the appearance that they have a relationship with God by staying in the church. A lukewarm Christian is like a lobster that doesn't know that it's about to be cooked. The water in the pot is lukewarm, which feels comfortable to it, but then the chef gradually turns up the heat until it's too late for the lobster to jump out. That's how the devil manipulates lukewarm Christians. He gradually turns up the heat while you are in your comfort zone, until it's too late for you to escape. But you do not have to stay in that lukewarm state. God always gives you a way of escaping, but you've got to listen and obey.

At one time, Gentiles, you did not know God, until He poured out His Spirit on you. Now the Holy Spirit is supposed to teach you how to live for God and abstain from fornication, drugs, drunkenness, adultery, and so on. Gentiles, you really do not have an excuse for your sinful action. The devil does not want you to be sanctified and set apart from sin. Why is it that every time we watch television or read a newspaper, we hear about God's people getting caught in sexual misconduct? People are getting caught up in these things because they are walking in the sleep in sin. "The Lord calls none into his family to live unholy lives, but that they may be taught and enabled to walk before him in holiness. Some make light of the precepts of holiness, because they hear them from men; but they are God's commands, and to break them is to despise God."⁹ God did not call you back to impurity, but to holiness. He said that you should be holy because He is Holy.

Allow God to orchestrate the events of your life each and every day. Even if your plans are thwarted, continue to seek God. Even if you think that everything is going smoothly in your life, be cognizant of God's sovereign presence, because He is always with you. Have you ever wondered why God says in Deuteronomy 31:6 that He will never forsake us? The answer is in 1 Samuel 12:2: "For the Lord will not forsake his people, for his great name's sake, because it has pleased the Lord to make you a people for himself"(ESV). God said that it gives Him great pleasure to make you His. God wants all of you—not just part of you—but that means that you must stop walking in the sleep in sin. "The eternal God is your dwelling place, and underneath are the everlasting arms. And he thrust out the enemy before you and said, 'Destroy'" (Deuteronomy 33:27). God wants to annihilate your enemy, if you'll allow Him to do so.

God won't let anything separate you from Him, as long as you remain in Christ Jesus. "For I am sure that neither death nor life, nor angels nor rulers, nor things present nor things to come, nor powers, nor height nor depth, nor anything else in all creation, will be able to separate us from the love of God in Christ Jesus our Lord" (Romans 8:38–39 KJV).

So, church, it's way past time to awaken and put on your war clothes. It's time to do battle in the Spirit realm, so that your children can be set free from living in bondage. "And have cast lots for my people, and have traded a boy for a prostitute, and have sold a girl for wine and have drunk it" (Joel 3:3 KJV). It's time for the church to be set free from bondage to the devil. You must wake up and stop turning over your children to slavery, prostitution, drugs, drunkenness, and sexual immorality in Jesus's name. "Proclaim this among the nations: Consecrate for war; stir up the mighty men. Let all the men of war draw near; let them come up" (Joel 3:9 KJV).

If you remain in uncleanness and keep walking down the sleep in sin path, then be prepared to be like the five foolish virgins.

NINE

Five Foolish Virgins

How do you know if you have not awakened? Is it when you aren't prepared, like the five foolish virgins? How much longer should you sleep in sin while the bridegroom tarries? Jesus spoke to the people in parables about God's kingdom in heaven, and then he told the parable of the ten virgins. Jesus talked about how the ten virgins took their lamps with them to meet the bridegroom. Five of the virgins were wise, but the other five were foolish because they planned poorly and weren't prepared for the bridegroom, who tarried. The word *tarry* means to delay or be tardy in acting or doing; to linger in expectation. (Read Matthew 25:1–13 and take heed.)

The ten virgins had twelve things in common:

1. All were virgins keeping their ways pure before the Lord, because they knew that virginity belongs to God.
2. All belonged to a church.
3. All had Christian biblical beliefs. They were all waiting on the bridegroom.
4. All bought their own lamps.
5. All bought their own Bibles. This is a figure of speech that applies to modern Christians.
6. All went to meet the bridegroom, though they didn't know when He would come.
7. All looked forward to the Second Coming of Jesus Christ.
8. All fell asleep, since the bridegroom tarried.

9. All arose from their sleep when they heard the angel announce that the bridegroom had arrived.
10. All prepared their lamps by trimming the wicks.
11. All the lamps were still burning.
12. All were in agreement about meeting the bridegroom.

One of the main differences between the five foolish virgins and the five wise virgins is that the foolish virgins didn't plan ahead nor did they bring a flask of oil with their lamps, so they were burning the previous day's oil. When Jesus, the bridegroom, returns for the church, he is going to be looking for the Holy Spirit, which is symbolized by the lamp oil, residing in us. Jesus doesn't want to hear that yesterday's oil is in our lamps, because yesterday's oil isn't good enough. Jesus wants us to be burning fresh anointing oil from the Holy Spirit.

We have come too far, church, to turn back now. So keep asking God for a fresh anointing of His Holy Spirit each and every day to keep your lamp burning strong. We need the kind of oil that flowed from Aaron's beard: "It is like the precious oil on the head, running down on the beard, on the beard of Aaron, running down on the collar of his robes!" (Psalm 133:2) "And he poured some of the anointing oil on Aaron's head and anointed him to consecrate him" (Leviticus 8:12 KJV). We need the oil of the Holy Spirit to saturate us from the crowns of our heads to the soles of our feet. We need to be transparent so the world can see the Holy Spirit residing in us.

Another difference was that Jesus didn't know the five foolish virgins because they simply attended church, but the wise virgins knew that they *were* the church. The foolish virgins were caught up in tradition and religion; they didn't have a personal relationship with Jesus like the wise virgins did. The five foolish virgins weren't allowed to enter the building where the marriage feast was held; they just stood there pounding on the locked door. "Afterward the other virgins came also, saying, 'Lord, lord, open to us.' But he answered, 'Truly, I say to you, I do not know you.'" (Matthew 25:11–12 KJV). The five foolish virgins appeared to be walking and living right, but they didn't know how to ask for fresh anointing oil from the Holy Spirit.

Church, you cannot buy the Holy Spirit or get it from someone else. The Holy Spirit is a free gift when you accept Jesus Christ as your Lord and Savior. All you have to do is ask Him to pour out His Spirit upon you, and He will do it. When you pretend that you have the Holy Spirit living inside, you're only fooling yourself, like the five foolish virgins. It's so easy to let your oil burn out when you are sleeping in sin. The Bible is full of stories meant to inspire you to get closer to God. The Word of God says that if you remain in sleep in sin, God will tell you to depart from Him, because He never knew you. But if you wake up and remain in Jesus, He will remain in you.

If the Holy Spirit, your comforter, doesn't live inside you, then you can say all day long, "Lord, Lord, open to us," but Jesus will reply, "I knew you not." I implore you to ensure that your oil is replenished on a daily basis. Do not be caught unprepared at the midnight hour when Jesus returns for His church. Those five foolish virgins were lukewarm, caught up in attending church and going through the religious motions, but really just straddling the fence. They thought that a little dab of oil would get them into the bridegroom's feast, but they got a rude awakening. Church, a little dab will get you shut out of the feast and spewed out of Jesus's mouth.

How does Old Testament oil compare to New Testament oil? In the Old Testament, anointing oil was pure, beaten olive oil that was burned in lamps inside the tabernacle. Anointing oil was used to consecrate everything inside the tabernacle. For many generations, every time a priest entered the tabernacle, he had to be consecrated by being sprinkled with anointing oil so that he would be holy in the presence of God. In the New Testament, oil comes through accepting Jesus Christ as your Lord and Savior, but it doesn't stop there. Jesus said that when He went to the Father, He wouldn't leave us comfortless, and our comforter is the Holy Spirit.

While the ten virgins were waiting for the bridegroom to arrive, I believe that they were singing spiritual songs and praising God. The five wise virgins had the balm of Gilead oil flowing inside of them, but the five foolish virgins didn't have a true personal relationship with Jesus Christ. They were trying to get into the feast on the coattails of the five wise virgins.

"Many will say to Me in that day, 'Lord, Lord, have we not prophesied in Your name, cast out demons in Your name, and done many wonders in Your name?' And then I will declare to them, 'I never knew you, depart from Me, you who practice lawlessness!'" (Matthew 7:22–23 ESV). Everything those people did was done in vain for their own glorification, because they had allowed pride to creep into their lives. At one time they had been on fire for God, but then they started listening to the enemy's voice telling their flesh, "You performed these miracles in your own strength." They lost their personal relationship with Jesus Christ, because no flesh that includes pride, arrogance, or selfishness can dwell in the presence of God.

It's time-out for these phony relationships and time to stop playing church. Your relationship with Jesus has to be personal. God's people are supposed to be the church. You need to stop saying one thing and doing another; instead, you need to practice what you preach. Are you going to church just for show and to please other people, like the Pharisees and Sadducees did? Is so, then that's your reward. I don't know about you, but I want to hear these words from Jesus: "Well done, My faithful servant." The choice is yours. You're going to hear either "Well done, My faithful servant" or "Depart from me, for I never knew you."

I implore you to awaken, because your life is hanging in the balance. This is not a joke. People are dying every day without having accepted Jesus as their Lord and Savior. "I knew Jesus when I was a child" is old oil that won't get you into the bridegroom's feast. So repent and start building a personal relationship with Him today. You have easy access to the Father. Can I tell you something? The devil does not want you to repent, but you can be restored.

If you're a single Christian who has lost your virginity, repent before the Lord and remain celibate. Jesus is coming back for a church without spots and blemishes. When I was single, I wasn't faithful to the Lord. I did my own thing to please the flesh, instead of walking with God.

I remember a time when I was angry with God. During my senior year of college, I had emergency surgery for a bleeding ulcer and I didn't know exactly what was going on. I lost at least three pints of blood and almost bled to death. That was a scary and trying time for me, and I remember lying on the hospital table and praying. I bargained with God that if He spared my life, I would serve Him all of my life. God held up His end of the bargain, but I didn't. Have you ever made a bargain with God and then not held up your end of the bargain? Because of the surgery, I had to delay graduating from college, which meant that I had to decline a job offer from NASA. Little did I know that the devil was feeding me lies: "Look what God did to you. You almost died in the hospital. What kind of God does that to His child?" I was getting more and more angry with God.

So I started doing my own thing, going to parties and playing Russian roulette with the devil. I kept going to church and living a religious life, but I was just going through the motions. When it came to winning souls for Jesus, I was ineffective and just fooling myself. I didn't have any anointing oil in my life, so my light was gradually getting dimmer. I was definitely like the five foolish virgins. If Jesus, the bridegroom, had come while I was sleeping in sin, I would have found myself knocking at the door and begging Him to let me in. But thanks be to God, who leads us to triumph, He loved me and didn't want me to remain asleep in Sin Dungeon. Jesus doesn't want us to miss the marriage feast. We serve a merciful and just God. All we have to do is repent.

Praise be to God, I woke up and started serving Him again. The Bible tells us to repent, but also to remember falling. Church, we need to put on our whole armor so we can perpetually fight off those fiery darts, which the enemy keeps bombarding us with. The devil will keep telling you that you're unworthy, that you'll never amount to anything, that you'll always be a drunk, drug addict, prostitute, pervert, and so on. You need to stop listening to that old devil and his word curses. I'm here to tell you that you *are* worthy and that you *can* become everything that God has called you to be. Don't let the devil convince you that your current lifestyle is who you are. You are a mighty person of valor in Jesus's name. In fact, you're the very reason why Jesus came—to save people just like you, whom the world has thrown out like trash. This is His amazing grace, and how sweet is the sound that saves wretches like you and me. I once was lost, but now I'm found. I was blindly sleeping in sin, but now I've awakened and I see. Hallelujah! Glory to God!

The church, Jesus's bride, needs to be prepared for the return of the bridegroom, Jesus Christ, and the big wedding feast. It is high time to clean up and put our house in order for Jesus. The devil is mad, and he's trying to hinder us from being prepared to meet the bridegroom. The devil

When isn't Christ in us? I've read some serious words about this. But before I mention them, I want to point out some things from which we can free ourselves by living a life with the Holy Spirit. *Matthew Henry's Concise Commentary* says, "A spirit contrary to the spirit of Christ would deny Him, whatever the profession. Men may deny Christ by evil speaking, by foolish talking, by words that are untruthful or unkind. They may deny Him by shunning life's burdens, by the pursuit of sinful pleasure. They may deny Him by conforming to the world, by uncourteous behavior, by the love of their own opinions, by justifying self, by cherishing doubt, borrowing trouble, and dwelling in darkness. In all these ways they declare that Christ is not in them."

All ten virgins prepared and lit their lamps, but burning lamps need oil. After a short time, five of the virgins noticed that their lamps were going out. The lamps of the foolish virgins did burn for a while, which tells us that they had some of the Holy Spirit, but it wasn't enough. Their lamps had too little oil. The church needs a fresh anointing of oil from the Holy Spirit every day—not just once a week. We can't afford to run out of oil; a little dab will not get us into heaven. None of us wants to hear Jesus say the words "I never knew you."

Jesus's words tell us that our personal relationship with Him has something to do with the Holy Spirit. People who don't let themselves be led by the Holy Spirit won't be acknowledged by Jesus. Romans 8:8–9 says, "Those who are in the flesh cannot please God. If anyone does not have the Spirit of Christ, he is not His." These are God's words, not mine.

Actually, we can have a real, personal relationship with Jesus only through the Holy Spirit. First John 3:24 says, "And by this we know that He [Jesus] abides in us, by the Spirit whom He has given us." When we are filled with the Holy Spirit, we can rest assured that we are in Jesus, too, and He is in us.

Romans 8:9b says, "Now if anyone does not have the Spirit of Christ, he is not His." This scripture shocked me, just as it should shock the church. If you refuse to accept the Holy Spirit, you are grieving Him. Are you sure that you have accepted the Holy Spirit and that He is working in you? Or are you painfully missing the Spirit's "fruits" in your life? I pray that you will have a deep desire to receive the Holy Spirit, that your heart will be changed, and that God the Father will change you according to His will.

How do you know that you are not awakening? When you think that it's all right to be a carnal Christian. The greatest tragedy for the carnal Christian is that he won't receive eternal life if his condition doesn't change. Romans 8:9b says, "Now if anyone does not have the Spirit of Christ, he is not His." The main difference between spiritual and carnal church members has to do with the Holy Spirit. The spiritual Christian is led by the Holy Spirit. When you finally awaken and realize that you are behaving like a carnal Christian, don't be angry. God offers you a remedy in the Holy Spirit.

The Holy Spirit is overemphasized in some circles and neglected in others. May the Lord lead us on the path to the Biblical middle. A. W. Tozer said, "If the Holy Spirit was withdrawn from the church today, 95 percent of what we do would go on and no one would know the difference. If the Holy Spirit had been withdrawn from the New Testament church, 95 percent of what they did would stop, and everybody would know the difference."[11] Pastor, if your church is operating this way, then you are running a dead church. In everything that you do, the Holy Spirit should be your guide. At every service, you should pray that the Holy Spirit has free rein in every aspect of the church's operations and inside the sanctuary. The church is not an organization—it's a complex organism. There is hope for the church if we walk by faith and not by sight. "Now faith is the assurance of things hoped for, the conviction of things not seen" (Hebrews 11:1).

I can testify that there is power in the name of Jesus to break every chain and set you free from bondage. On April 28, 1994, my wife had a spiritual awakening and God showed her His plan for our lives. She rejoiced with praise and thanksgiving. God revealed to her that He was still in control of our lives, and that we were where He had planted us to be. We were living in the city of Warner Robins, Georgia, at the time of her awakening. I believe that God was revealing to her that we are living in the latter days and showing her the new church that He's establishing. As long as we remain willing vessels for His use, this new church will be built on the true foundation, which is Jesus Christ. It is past time for us to wake up and be on fire for God. (Read Deuteronomy 9:3, 4:24, and Hebrews 12:28–29.) Hebrews 12:28 says, "Wherefore we receiving a kingdom which cannot be moved, let us have grace, whereby we may serve God acceptably with reverence and godly fear."

Isaiah 43:18 says, "We are to forget those things which are behind." Repent and leave the past at the foot of the cross. You cannot change your past, but you can repent and ask forgiveness. If you confess your sins, He is faithful and just to cleanse you from all unrighteousness. Learn how to use your past as a stepping-stone and not as a stumbling block. The heart is desperately wicked. Who should know it but God? That's another reason why you should keep your mind on Him.

If you have escaped the enemy's snares, then you should be walking in the hope of Jesus Christ. If you're walking in hope, you'll be protected from depression and self-pity. Hope is like a golden cord connected to heaven. The more you cling to this cord, the more God will bear the weight of your burdens and you'll feel lighter. Neither God's kingdom nor His plans for you are heavy. If you'll cling to His hope and His Son, then rays of light will reach you through the darkness.

During the College Football Playoff championship game on January 8, 2018, Tua Tagovailoa, the second-string quarterback at the University of Alabama, was put in by Coach Nick Saban in the second half of the game. Georgia didn't know anything about him, and Tagovailoa led the Crimson Tide to an overtime victory. During his post-game interview with the sports media, Tagovailoa gave all the glory to Jesus Christ, mentioning Jesus's name several times. The interview was broadcast live, so nothing was beeped out—but Tagovailoa didn't care if he offended anyone by saying the name of Jesus Christ. The enemy knows that there is power in the name of Jesus; that's why he doesn't want us to use it.

How do you know if you have not yet been awakened? You're stuck in a negative frame of mind and cannot see Jesus or His gifts. If you can't rise above negative thoughts, try to program your mind to thank Him through faith. "Father, I thank you for these thoughts that are preoccupying my mind today. You said that You will keep me in perfect peace if my mind stays on You. I choose today to break the cycle of negative thoughts. I choose today to trust you and to walk by faith, not by sight or how I'm feeling." If you do this every morning, it will clear the blockage and you'll find Jesus in the midst of your storm.

The devil's job is to keep you powerless by lulling you into a deep sleep. If you believe, however, the devil can't keep you from being filled and used by the Holy Spirit. On the contrary, this should provide every opportunity for His power to shine forth brighter than the sun in your life. "For thus said the Lord God, the Holy One of Israel, 'In returning and rest you shall be saved; in quietness and in trust shall be your strength'" (Isaiah 30:15a ESV).

"'Is not my word like as a fire?' saith the Lord; 'and like a hammer that breaketh the rock in pieces?'" (Jeremiah 23:29 KJV). God broke up their hearts of stone and shattered them into pieces. Jeremiah said that God's Word was like fire shut up in his bones. "Then I said, 'I will not make mention of him, nor speak any more in his name.' But his word was in mine heart as a burning fire shut up in my bones, and I was weary with forbearing, and I could not stay" (Jeremiah 20:9 KJV).

Did you know that sleeping in sin will make your life mundane and keep you from being on fire for God? God does not want us to be lukewarm. He wants us to be on fire for Him. We need to lead lives that are pleasing in God's sight, which means telling this dying world about Jesus. Life is nothing but a vapor—we're here one minute and gone the next. The Father wants you to wake up so that you won't think that you're a prima donna.

~ TEN ~

Prima Donna

If you stay in the devil's slumber, you'll begin to act like a prima donna or popinjay. You'll believe that you are better than others, and you'll act supercilious toward other races. The church will be puffed up, arrogant, vain, and shallow. The devil will have deceived you into thinking that one race of people is superior to another race. If you have that mind-set, I beseech you to wake up in Jesus's name. We were all created in His image, regardless of our skin color. Red, yellow, black, and white are all precious in His sight. We're supposed to be Jesus's mouthpiece regardless of the color of our skin.

We need to see people the way God sees them, as fearfully and wonderfully made. (Read Psalm 139:14.) He sees them as the apple of His eye. (Read Psalm 17:8.) He sees them as royal priests, ambassadors for Jesus Christ. "But ye are a chosen generation, a royal priesthood, a holy nation, a peculiar people; that ye should shew forth the praises of him who hath called you out of darkness into his marvelous light" (1 Peter 2:9 KJV). The church includes the highest-ranking people because we represent Jesus Christ. I pray that the church will come to understand this and start walking like royalty, rather than in arrogance and pride. If you think that you're a prima donna, then you need to stop listening to the devil, who is telling you these lies.

What about people who have low self-esteem? You need to stop listening to the lies of the devil, who tells you that you're nothing more than trash. Don't even entertain those thoughts. Jesus said that you are worthy, and that's why He came to this earth to save the lost. Stand in front of a mirror and tell yourself, "I am worthy. I am a royal priest, an ambassador for Jesus Christ, and God says that I am holy." Ephesians 1:4 says, "Even as he chose us in him before the foundation of the world, that we should be holy and blameless before him" (ESV). Align your thoughts with the Word of God. Even before the world existed, God chose you to walk in holiness. "But as he who called you is holy, you also be holy in all your conduct, since it is written, 'You shall be holy, for I am holy'" (1 Peter 1:15–16 ESV).

If you continue to sleep in sin and think that you're a prima donna, your conduct won't be holy. You'll just please your flesh and be at the devil's beck and call. So keep repeating the scriptures until they become engraved on your heart, and then you'll know that you have stopped listening to the lies of the enemy and your flesh. If you keep that flesh on the cross where it belongs, then you'll remain humble and not act like a popinjay. You have a powerful weapon to use against the devil—the name of Jesus. When you speak the name of Jesus, it's so powerful that the devil has to flee. That's why the church has to wake up.

The Bible says that if you hate your brother and think you're better than those who are in Christ Jesus, then you're a murderer and sleeping in sin. I didn't call you a murderer—God did. "Everyone who hates his brother is a murderer, and you know that no murderer has eternal life abiding in him" (1 John 3:15 ESV). God is adamant about loving your brother. Why do you let prejudicial ignorance separate you from God? Is hating your brother worth being separated from God?

How can you be forgiven if you continue to hate your brother? How can there be remission of sin if you continue to show prejudicial ignorance? Without the shedding of blood, there is no forgiveness of sin. Redemption and salvation come through the blood of Jesus Christ. "Indeed, under the law almost everything is purified with blood, and without the shedding of blood there is no forgiveness of sins" (Hebrews 9:22). Jesus wants to blot out your sins and throw them into the sea of forgetfulness.

"I am he who blots out your transgressions for my own sake, and I will not remember your sins" (Isaiah 43:25). Do you know that when you act like a prima donna, you think that your thoughts are purer than God? They go hand in hand with each other.

∽ ELEVEN ∾

Thoughts Purer Than God's

How do you know if you are not awakening? You think that your thoughts are purer than the thoughts of God, your maker. "Can mortal man be in the right before God? Can a man be pure before his Maker?" (Job 4:17 KJV) "Shall a weak, sinful, dying creature, pretend to be more just than God, and more pure than his Maker? Of course not!"[12] When you don't acknowledge God in all your ways, you'll think that your fleshly ways are higher than God's ways and your fleshly thoughts are higher than God's thoughts. This stinking, ludicrous way of thinking is completely contrary to God, but the devil wants us to keep up this backward thinking, like Adam and Eve did in the garden. "For my thoughts are not your thoughts, neither are your ways my ways, declares the Lord. For as the heavens are higher than the earth, so are my ways higher than your ways and my thoughts than your thoughts" (Isaiah 55:8–9).

Staying in that deep sleep-in-sin pit will cause you to lean on your own understanding rather than on God's understanding. God wants to direct your path, if you'll just wake up and acknowledge Him in all your ways. "Trust in the Lord with all thine heart; and lean not unto thine own understanding. In all thy ways acknowledge him, and he shall direct thy paths" (Proverbs 3:5–6 KJV). You should never let your flesh guide you, because it will lead you down the road to destruction.

God knows the secrets of your heart, so don't try to hide them from Him. "Would not God discover this? For he knows the secrets of the heart" (Psalm 44:21 ESV). Don't let the devil trick you into thinking that God doesn't know everything about you. God knew when I was living in sin. Sometimes you think that others don't know, but usually you're just fooling yourself. God doesn't want you to have secret sins. If you confess your sins, He is faithful and just to cleanse you from all unrighteousness. "Notwithstanding the seeming impunity of men for a short time, though living without God in the world, their doom is as certain as that of the villainy angels, and is continually overtaking them."[13] It is high time to wake up, because it's too dangerous to live on this earth without God.

"Amid thoughts from visions of the night, when deep sleep falls on men" (Job 4:13 ESV). It is difficult to hear God speaking to you when you're in the devil's sleep in sin. In Proverbs 6:9, God asks, "How long will you sleep, O Sluggard?" "When will you arise out of your sleep? When will you be awakening? How many love their sleep in sin, and their dreams of worldly happiness! Shall we not seek to awaken such? Shall we not give diligence to secure our own salvation?"[14]

When I was asleep in sin, I stayed away from the light. I wanted to keep my sleep in sin hidden from other Christians, because the devil told me that they would be judgmental. The church acts like there are small sins and big sins, but in God's eyes, sin is sin. So church, instead of judging people, just love them and let them know that they aren't alone. Talk about how God delivered you and changed your life. Let people know that God called you out of darkness into His marvelous light. Let them know that they are beloved by the Father and you.

A sluggard is a habitually lazy person. God wants you to snap out of the deep sleep-in-sin spell that the devil has you under. If your thoughts are not focused on Jesus Christ, then you're still sleeping. God wants to keep you in perfect peace, but your mind has to be consumed by thoughts of Him. The devil wants you to keep sleeping in the sleep in sin so that you'll fall to your death. In Acts 20:9, Euthychus allowed the enemy to put him into a deep sleep while Paul was preaching. Unfortunately Euthychus was sitting in a windowsill on the third floor, so when he went to sleep, he fell out of the window and was killed. But Paul ran down to him and fell on Euthychus to revive him.

When your mind wanders during a service, you're letting the enemy put you into a deep sleep. I'm guilty of that. The enemy doesn't want you to hear what the Lord is saying through your pastor, because it might set you free. My wife has asked me several times if I heard what the pastor said about this or that, and I've had to admit that I missed it. People retain only 10 percent of what they hear, which is why I take notes when my pastor is speaking. That way, I can go back and think about the message again, even though sometimes it takes discipline to go back and read those notes. If you're like me, you are wondering what's for lunch, or if you unplugged the iron, or whether your favorite football team is playing on television. My mind wanders and I get sleepy when I'm praying or reading my Bible. I have to catch myself when I get distracted and put my mind back on God. It's easy to be preoccupied by life and let our minds wander. But if we don't learn to control our thoughts, we will see evil recompensed for good.

~ TWELVE ~

Evil Recompensed for Good

How do you know if you are not awakening? If you think that evil will be recompensed for good, then you aren't waking up. "Shall evil be recompensed for good? For they have dug a pit for my soul. Remember that I stood before thee to speak good for them, and to turn away thy wrath from them" (Jeremiah 18:20 KJV). If your flesh believes that evil is good and good is evil, and you start embracing such stinking thoughts, then woe to you! When you harden your heart against the things of God, you'd better look out.

God told Jeremiah, his major prophet, to go down to the potter's house to hear His words. While Jeremiah was at the potter's house, he noticed that when a vessel made from clay became marred in the potter's hand, the potter made another vessel. That's how God spoke to Jeremiah and told him what to say to Israel. God told him to say that just like the potter did to that marred vessel, God could destroy Israel and start over.

If you do what is evil in God's sight, thinking that evil is good, and you also disobey God's voice, then you'd better look out. God's Word says that obedience is better than sacrifice, and He commands us to obey Him. If you disobey God, He will frame evil against you and devise (imagine) a device against you. God will tell you to repent from your evil ways, like He did the Israelites, and He'll give you ample time to repent. But if you continue to harden your heart, then God will do to you the same thing the potter did to the marred clay vessel—He'll destroy you and start over. If you say, "It's in vain; for we will walk after our own devices," then God will turn you over to your reprobate mind. If you remain in your stubbornness and continue with your evil-hearted ways, then beware the consequences.

Jeremiah 18:21 says, "Therefore deliver up their children to the famine, and pour out their blood by the force of the sword; and let their wives be bereaved of their children, and be widows; and let their men be put to death; let their young men be slain by the sword in battle." Do you really want this to happen to you? This is happening in our schools today—they have become battlegrounds. We need to wake up and run back to God in Jesus's name, so that all this madness will stop!

Let's dissect Jeremiah 18:21. "Turn them over to the power of the sword" could mean that you die in your sins because you have no umbrella of protection. "When the prophet called to repentance, instead of obeying the call, the people devised devices against him. Thus do sinners deal with the great Intercessor, crucifying him afresh, and speaking against him on earth, while his blood is speaking for them in heaven. But the prophet had done his duty to them; and the same will be our rejoicing in a day of evil."[15]

We are losing too many of our children to the power of the sword—drugs, alcohol, pornography, sex, car accidents, and greed, as well as active shooters in our schools. The church needs to say, "Enough is enough. Stop this madness!" The church needs to repent, turn from their wicked ways, and say, "As for me and my house, we will once again serve the Lord." It's not too late to start serving Him again. We need to seek the Lord while He can be found. If we let our hearts get harder and harder, it will be difficult to find Him.

God doesn't want us to remain in captivity or in a deep sleep-in-sin pit. He wants us to be free from bondage so that we can return to the Promised Land. The shootings in our schools are grieving our heavenly Father. When His children die by the sword, it grieves Him. When His children harden their hearts, it grieves Him. If the church doesn't repent, then they will remain religious and continue to adopt legalism, and then our children will not be protected.

PART THREE

Religious Spirit

~ THIRTEEN ~

A Spirit of Legalism/Religion

How do you know if you are sleeping in satan's sin dungeon? You realize you are being controlled by a legalistic religious spirit and didn't even know it. Some of you might be offended by this chapter, especially if you're not ready to let go of legalism. Religious legalism involves obeying the dos and don'ts, instead of obeying God. For example, legalism says that you cannot heal on the Sabbath. The devil will try to trick you into thinking that legalistic religion will get you into heaven, but it won't. Instead, legalism will keep you locked up in that sleep in Sin Dungeon. Even if the Pharisees and Sadducees came back to earth and told you that religion and legalism wouldn't get you into heaven, you probably still wouldn't believe them.

Remember the story about the rich man and Lazarus? Lazarus died and went to heaven, but the rich man went to hell. The rich man asked Abraham if Lazarus could stick his finger in the water to cool the rich man's tongue, because he was being tormented in the flames of hell. Then the rich man asked Abraham to let someone go and warn his five brothers: "And he said, 'Then I beg you, father, to send him to my father's house— for I have five brothers—so that he may warn them, lest they also come into this place of torment.' But Abraham said, 'They have Moses and the Prophets; let them hear them.' And he said, 'No, father Abraham, but if someone goes to them from the dead, they will repent.' He said to him, 'If they do not hear Moses and the Prophets, neither will they be convinced if someone should rise from the dead'" (Luke 16:27–31 ASV).

If you aren't listening to the Word of God, His pastors, and His prophets, then you have allowed religion and legalism to harden your heart:

> And the ruler of the synagogue answered with indignation, because that Jesus had healed on the Sabbath day, and said unto the people, There are six days in which men ought to work: in them therefore come and be healed, and not on the Sabbath day. The Lord then answered him, and said, Thou hypocrite, doth not each one of you on the Sabbath loose his ox or his ass from the stall, and lead him away to watering? And ought not this woman, being a daughter of Abraham, whom satan hath bound, lo, these eighteen years, be loosed from this bond on the Sabbath day? And when he had said these things, all his adversaries were ashamed: and all the people rejoiced for all the glorious things that were done by him. (Luke 13:14–17 KJV)

Jesus knew the hearts of the Pharisees and Sadducees, and He refused to allow that spirit of religion to control Him. "According to Robert Stearns' research, Islam has set out to create an empire that includes not just Israel and the Middle East, but Europe and the Americas as well."[16] If America does not have a great spiritual awakening soon, the United States could be a Muslim and Islamic territory in a relatively short time.

If you can't get loose from a religious spirit, ask the Holy Spirit to give you the keys that you need to break free. God didn't call us back into bondage or to lay a foundation that's different from the truth of freedom foundation. If someone told you that you had a monkey on your back, but you couldn't feel or see it, would you believe them? The enemy has blinded you from the truth:

> According to the grace of God given to me, like a skilled master builder I laid a foundation, and someone else is building upon it. Let each one take care how he builds upon it. For no one can lay a foundation other than that which is laid, which is Jesus Christ. Now if anyone builds

> on the foundation with gold, silver, precious stones, wood, hay, straw each one's work will become manifest, for the Day will disclose it, because it will be revealed by fire, and the fire will test what sort of work each one has done. If the work that anyone has built on the foundation survives, he will receive a reward. If anyone's work is burned up, he will suffer loss, though he himself will be saved, but only as through fire. (1 Corinthians 3:10–15 ESV)

We are living in a time of forced political correctness, but I don't want to be politically correct—I want to be biblically correct. We're afraid of offending people, but people are listening to the voice of the enemy. The enemy will tell you that it's okay to do drugs; you won't become addicted (despite 121 overdoses per day on opioids). It's fine to drink; you won't become an alcoholic. It's all right to watch pornography one time; you won't get hooked. It's okay to want more stuff; you deserve it, and it won't make you crave more.

This sounds familiar, doesn't it? Remember in the garden of Eden, when satan spoke with Eve? He told her that she wouldn't die if she ate from the Tree of Knowledge of Good and Evil. In Genesis 2:16, God gave Adam only one commandment—not to eat from the Tree of Knowledge of Good and Evil, or he would surely die. God is omnipresent, so why did He put that tree in the middle of the garden? God knew that satan and his demons, who had been kicked out of heaven, were roaming freely on earth. Why didn't God send the devil and his demons to Mars or some other planet?

God created us with a free will, so we will always have to reckon with our flesh. God doesn't tempt us—He only tests us. Eve came on the scene *after* Adam had been given the commandment, so she got it secondhand from him and probably got it all mixed up. In Genesis 3:1–5, Eve had a conversation with the devil in the form of a serpent. Eve told the serpent that she and Adam could eat fruit from any tree except the one in the middle of the garden, but that God had warned them that if they ate the fruit from that tree, or even just touched it, they would die. satan then told a lie on God—the first lie told on earth—when he said that God was wrong and that eating from that tree wouldn't kill Adam and Eve.

When you talk with that cunning devil about the Word of God, be careful that he doesn't trip you up. The devil knows the Word probably better than you and I do, but he doesn't know how to live the Word of God, and that's why he got kicked out of heaven. The devil wanted to take over God's throne, but God doesn't share His throne with anyone. Stop talking with the devil and start having conversations with God, the lover of your soul, who created you in His image.

Everything began in the garden of Eden. Adam was placed in the garden of Eden to tend to it. What language did Adam and Eve speak? God created every language under the sun, but no matter what language Adam and Eve spoke, the devil was able to talk with them.

Staying in the devil's sleep in Sin Dungeon will make you hide in the dark, because the light will expose things that you and the devil don't want exposed. In Genesis 3:9, Adam and Eve heard the voice of God in the garden and they were afraid. Their eyes were opened to good and evil, and they knew that they were naked so they tried to hide from God. Sin will cloud your thinking until you cannot think clearly. God knew exactly where Adam and Eve were hiding and what they had done.

After they sinned against God, Adam and Eve could've either repented or eaten from the Tree of Life. God gives us ample time to repent of our sin, and if Adam and Eve had just repented, God would have forgiven them, but their minds were too clouded and confused. They also could have eaten from the Tree of Life, but they didn't think about that either. God did not tell them that they couldn't eat from the Tree of Life. "And the Lord God commanded the man, saying, 'You may surely eat of every tree of the garden, but of the tree of the knowledge of good and evil you shall not eat, for in the day that you eat of it you shall surely die'" (Genesis 2:16–17).

We are no different today, when we dabble in things that we shouldn't be doing. After we sin, we often try to hide because of our shame and guilt, but that's still the trick of the devil. The devil is not creative and his tricks are just illusions, like David Copperfield working with smoke and mirrors. God said, "If we confess our sins, He is faithful and just to forgive us our sins and to cleanse us from all unrighteousness" (1 John 1:9). He didn't say *some* of our unrighteousness, but *all* of it. The only thing we have to do is to confess.

Why didn't the devil tell Eve to eat from the Tree of Life instead of the Tree of Knowledge of Good and Evil? Because He loathes God and wants to trip us up and make us disobey God. When God told Adam that he would surely die, He was talking about a spiritual death. Adam and Eve didn't die instantaneously after eating from the Tree of Knowledge of Good and Evil. When God breathed life into Adam, He also breathed His spirit into Adam.

When God called for Adam in the garden, He stayed calm and didn't raise His voice. And God started asking Adam questions, although He already knew the answers. "But the Lord God called to the man and said to him, 'Where are you?' And he said, 'I heard the sound of you in the garden, and I was afraid, because I was naked, and I hid myself.' He said, 'Who told you that you were naked? Have you eaten of the tree of which I commanded you not to eat?'" (Genesis 3:9–11). God did not give Adam the spirit of fear, so why was Adam afraid of God's voice? That wasn't the first time that Adam had heard God's voice, but sin will cause us to walk in fear.

While Adam and God were talking about what Adam had done, Adam started playing the blame game. It's easy to blame others instead of being accountable for our own actions. "The man said, 'The woman whom you gave to be with me, she gave me fruit of the tree, and I ate.' Then the Lord God said to the woman, 'What is this that you have done?' The woman said, 'The serpent deceived me, and I ate'" (Genesis 3:12–13). Can I be honest with you? God doesn't want to hear our excuses. He wants us to have repentant hearts.

Every day, we are given a choice. Do we choose to blame God for our bad decisions? "Well, God, You created me, so this is Your fault." That sounds ludicrous, right? Or do we choose to blame others? It's so easy to let somebody else be the fall guy. What about a drug addict who has a conversation with God? "Hey God, that person whom you brought into my life gave me those illegal drugs, so I took them." No, we need to take ownership of our own actions. If that drug addict had listened to God's voice, God would have told him to flee and not take those drugs. Instead, he listened to the voice of the devil saying, "Go ahead. Those drugs aren't going to hurt you." The devil is the father of lies, so do not be deceived. Talking about being deceived by the devil, a friend of mind asked me to include this in my book. Do you know that the government will pay for someone that does meth and/or opoid can go to a clinic to get their fix during their pregnancy? After the baby is born the government will give the baby some type of drug to ease their addiction. We have gotten to the point where we do not value the life of a newborn and the mother. Hearing this type of stories just breaks my heart. God's people need to wake-up and say enough is enough. They need to know that this is not the plan God have for them.

The devil comes to steal, kill, and destroy, but God will never tell you to do anything that could harm or destroy you. God gives us free will to make our own decisions, but He has also given us His Word to help us make wise decisions. So take a stand and say "No!" to the devil and anything harmful to your body. Also, stop blaming others for your actions. If you want to be set free from addiction, run to the tree of repentance and eat from the Tree of Life, which is Jesus Christ. That's why people aren't delivered from addictions to drugs, alcohol, pornography, and sexual immorality—they'd rather blame other people than just confess and repent. Jesus wants to take these lustful desires from you, but He won't force you to give them up. That has to be your choice.

Jesus is the only one who can redeem and restore us. God's Word tells us that He doesn't wish any of us to perish: "The Lord is not slow to fulfill his promise as some count slowness, but is patient toward you, not wishing that any should perish, but that all should reach repentance" (2 Peter 3:9). God's desire for you is found in Jeremiah 29:11: "'For I know the plans I have for you,' declares the Lord, plans for welfare and not for evil, to give you a future and a hope'" (ESV). This is the Lord's declaration for you. God has a purpose for your life, if you'll just wake up and believe in Jesus's name.

In Psalm 119:105, the Bible tells us that God's Word is a lamp unto our feet and a light unto our path, so God wants to order our steps through His Word. Let's suppose that you have two paths from which to choose. You know that down one path are poisonous vipers, scorpions, and poisonous spiders, and you know that the second path will take you to love, joy, peace, prosperity, success, and a better life. You'd choose the second path, right?

If you lead a child down the wrong path and cause them to sin, then woe unto you. If an adult introduces something bad to a child and causes them to sin, the wrath of God will fall upon that adult. "But whoever causes one of these little ones who believe in me to sin, it would be better for him to have a great millstone fastened around his neck and to be drowned in the depth of the sea" (Matthew 18:6 ESV).

Before satan deceived Eve in the garden of Eden, Adam and Eve were filled with thankfulness, happiness, and contentment. But then the devil tempted Eve by pointing her toward the one thing that was forbidden. He didn't tempt her in things that weren't forbidden, because that's not in his nature. The devil will always try to counteract God's commands. The garden of Eden was filled with luscious fruits, but rather than being thankful for the many good things that were freely available, Adam and Eve let the devil persuade them to partake of the one fruit that God had commanded them not to eat.

Are we any different from Adam and Eve when it comes to the devil's schemes? Of course not. As soon as the devil lulls us into disobeying God, he has us right where he wants you. When we give in to the devil's temptation and partake of forbidden fruit, we blatantly sin against God by disobeying Him. Church, we are not ignorant of the nature of our individual forbidden fruits, which include pornography, drugs, sexual immorality, greed, and so on. But we all must resist three things: lust of the flesh, lust of the eyes, and pride of life.

"And the Lord said to satan, The Lord rebuke you, O satan! The Lord who has chosen Jerusalem rebuke you! Is not this a brand plucked from the fire?" (Zechariah 3:2 ESV). God had given Zechariah a vision of Joshua, the high priest, standing before the angel of the Lord and satan standing there accusing him. "But when the archangel Michael, contending with the devil, was disputing about the body of Moses, he did not presume to pronounce a blasphemous judgment, but said, 'The Lord rebuke you'" (Jude 1:9 ESV). The archangel Michael, who was contending with the devil, told the devil that the Lord rebuked him. If it worked for Joshua and Michael, it will work for you and me.

When the devil tempts us to do one of the things that I just mentioned, we must tell him that the Lord already rebuked him, but we have to be awake for this to be effective. If we refuse to wake up, then we're pleasing the devil. If we want to be used by God, then we have to awaken. God cannot use us if our minds are preoccupied with fleshly desires. Also, if we focus on what we don't have or situations that displease us, our minds will become dark and our senses will be dulled. If we're not sober about the schemes of the enemy, he will gradually lure us into places that we don't want to go and show us things that we never thought we'd see.

The devil will take us to the mountaintop and say to us, "I'll give you all these things if you bow down and worship me." Do not bargain with the devil, because everything that he offers comes at a high price. The price for Adam and Eve was separation from God and spiritual death.

We should be saying, "Greater is Jesus Christ who is in me than he (the devil) who is in the world." Keep repeating those words and watch that old devil flee. The only way that the devil can get a strong hold over your life is if you open a door for him. For example, if you go to a fortuneteller, tarot card reader, or soothsayer, or if you're even curious about things such as witchcraft, then you're opening the door for him to come in. There are demons behind the scene assisting, but of course you cannot see them.

God's children should never sleepwalk through the day, because you will bump into an obstacle that will keep you from becoming everything that God created you to be. Then you'll feel sorry for yourself, and self-pity is a slimy, bottomless pit that drags you deeper and deeper until it's difficult to get back out. As you slide down into that pit of self-pity, you're on your way to depression and a profound darkness. I should know, because I've been inside that slimy pit of the devil.

In 1985, I experienced an epic depression during which the darkness was so profound that I didn't know if my mind was coming or going. I couldn't function and was ineffective at my job, and I stayed in that slimy lair of the devil for six years. How did I get there? I opened the door for the devil to torment me. I had been running from God because I wanted to fit into the world and do my own thing. I was like the prodigal son, living in sin while the devil tormented my mind. I started isolating myself, which was exactly what the devil wanted because then he was able to torment me. I'm alive today only because the Lord told the devil, "You cannot kill him."

I should have run to God-fearing believers for help, but the devil kept telling me that they would judge and condemn me because of my chosen lifestyle. Day and night, I tried to battle that demon using my own fleshly power, but of course that didn't work. Being seriously depressed is terrifying, because you feel hopeless and useless. The devil has a field day with your mind, convincing you that people won't understand. I wouldn't wish that kind of depression on my worst enemy. I was literally sleepwalking in the devil's dungeon. I convinced myself that I was playing the religious card well, but I didn't have other strong believers fooled. Judgmental toward others and myself, I was not walking in love because I didn't know how. The devil's slave can't walk in love. I was in a pit of self-pity and despair with plateaus of pride and self-will, because I had taken my eyes off Jesus. I was in grave danger, spiritually dead and separated from God, and I lived in the abyss of my despair.

However, God wants us to escape that state of mind and focus on Him. How did I get out of the devil's dungeon? I simply repented and asked God for forgiveness. My depression didn't instantly go away, but I noticed that the closer I got to God, the closer He got to me. So I started meditating on His Word and praying to Him every day until that depression was totally gone. You can escape the abyss of despair if you allow God to pull you out. God wants you to live in the light. He wants to cover you with His righteousness and walk with you down the path of life. (In the Jesus Calling Book: Enjoying Peace In His Presence by Sarah Young dated July 16 on page 208, it talks about how walking in self-pity is a slimy, bottomless pit. Once you fall in, you tend to go deeper and deeper into the mire. As you slide down those slippery walls, you're well on your way to depression, and where the darkness is profound).

Another reason why the Lord wants us to wake up is so that we can sing a new song to Him: "He brought me up also out of a horrible pit, out of the miry clay, and set my feet upon a rock, and established my goings. And he hath put a new song in my mouth, even praise unto our God: many shall see it, and fear, and shall trust in the Lord. Blessed is that man that maketh the Lord his trust, and respecteth not the proud, nor such as turn aside to lies" (Psalm 40:2–4 KJV).

When you walk in the light, you'll see things from God's perspective instead of your own, so let the light of His presence fill your mind. When you awaken, you won't squander your energy on petty things or problems, because you'll be walking in the light of His love. But if you refuse to awaken, you'll be allowing the devil to usurp your life and lead you astray.

If you aren't using the spiritual gifts that God has given you, then you are trapped in satan's slimy abyss. Don't try to use your fleshly strength to get out of it, because that won't work. You need to put on the whole armor of God every day and tell God that you are willing to be used by Him. God wants the church to awaken and walk in righteousness. "Be not deceived: evil communications corrupt good manners. Awake to righteousness, and sin not; for some have not the knowledge of God: I speak this to your shame" (1 Corinthians 15:33–34).

Run with endurance, don't faint, and lay aside every hindrance or weight that ensnares you. "Wherefore seeing we also are compassed about with so great a cloud of witnesses, let us lay aside every weight, and the sin which doth so easily beset us, and let us run with patience the race that is set before us, Looking unto Jesus the author and finisher of our faith; who for the joy that was set before him endured the cross, despising the shame, and is set down at the right hand of the throne of God" (Hebrews 12:1–2 KJV).

I was living my life unconsciously, making habitual responses to every situation. Dullness crept in to paralyze me. I was just sleepwalking through life, following well-worn paths through daily routines. But God didn't want me to continue circling in those deeply rutted paths. He wanted to lead me down fresh trails of adventure, revealing things to me that I didn't know. Without conscious awareness, I was counterproductive to my own spiritual growth.[17]

The devil will always gainsay what Jesus wants to do in your life. He gainsaid Adam and Eve in the garden of Eden, and he is still gainsaying today. You need to silence the voice of the enemy by rebuking him in Jesus's name.

If you are lulled into the devil's slumberous dungeon, you will be prey to his schemes and fiery darts. But if the church awakens, then we won't be susceptible to the devil's devices. The church will be prayed up and equipped with the Word of God. It's imperative that the church be sober and vigilant, because our adversary, the devil, is walking around like a roaring lion seeking whom he may devour.

When God called us out of darkness into His marvelous light, the church was like a motley crew of misfits. But that's okay because we're just pilgrims passing through. "And be not conformed to this world: but be ye transformed by the renewing of your mind, that ye may prove what is that good, and acceptable, and perfect, will of God" (Romans 12:2). It's not God's plan for the church to stay in the devil's slumberous dungeon, just conforming to this world. He wants us to awaken and focus on the race and the prize set before us. The church should be undaunted when facing satan's fiery darts—bold and courageous, mounting up on eagles' wings.

God wants you to awaken and stay in His presence, so that He can suffuse your soul with joy. God has revealed to us the path that we should take in life, if we'll just stay in His presence. "Thou wilt shew me the path of life: in thy presence is fullness of joy; at thy right hand there are pleasures for evermore" (Psalm 16:11).

How would you know if you've been lulled into the devil's slumberous dungeon? You have if you try—and I stress the word *try*—to manipulate God into doing what you want Him to do for you. God is not a genie in a bottle that you can summon up at your command. Sometimes we want to have our cake and eat it too.

When I was in the hospital fighting for my life, I told God that if He let me live, I would serve Him for the rest of my life. God did let me live, but I didn't hold up my end of the bargain. In fact, I got angry with God for allowing me to get sick in the first place. "I shall not die, but live, and declare the works of the Lord. The Lord hath chastened me sore: but he hath not given me over unto death" (Psalm 118:17–18 KJV). I was a senior at the University of Alabama with a job offer from NASA to start working in the summer of 1983. However, my illness forced me to drop some courses, which delayed my graduation, so I had to decline the job offer.

Now when I look back, I see that everything happened for a reason. If I had graduated that summer and taken that job with NASA, I would never have met my future wife. She got a job at Robins Air Force Base and started work on January 30, 1989. I had stayed home that day because of a bad storm, but when I got to work the next day, everyone told me that there was an Auburn graduate whom I needed to meet. I was an Alabama graduate, so why would I want to meet an Auburn graduate? But eventually I relented and went to meet her. When I walked up to her, she had her back to me, and when she turned around, I thought she was the most beautiful woman I had ever seen. It was love at first sight for me, like in the Garden of Eden when God created Eve from one of Adam's ribs. When Adam saw Eve for the first time, he said, "Wo-man" and saw that she was beautiful. My wife, too, is bone of my bones and flesh of my flesh. Why am I telling you this? So that you'll learn to trust God and let Him direct your path. He created you and knows everything about you, right down to the number of hairs on your head. That's how important you are to God.

This life can be difficult at times. God said that we will have trials and tribulations, but that we should be of good cheer, for Jesus has overcome the world. I don't know why God doesn't heal everyone, but I do know that He heals. I know that Jesus can raise people from the dead and that God can speak life back into dried-up bones. I don't know why some people don't get saved, but Jesus gives us free will to accept or not accept Him as Lord and Savior. Paul said, "For to me to live is Christ, and to die is gain" (Philippians 1:21 ESV).

I know that both heaven and hell exist, and that it's up to us to choose which one to go to. If we accept Jesus as Lord and Savior, we'll go to heaven and be with Him. But if we refuse to accept Him, then we'll be separated from Him forever. Why would we not want to be with the one who created us in His image and loves us very much. "For God so loved the world, that He gave His only begotten Son, that whosoever believeth in Him should not perish, but have everlasting life" (John 3:16 KJV).

But God didn't stop there: "For God sent not his Son into the world to condemn the world; but that the world through him might be saved" (John 3:17 KJV). God doesn't want any of us to perish, but to have everlasting life. Jesus didn't come to condemn us, but to save us. That's why He tells us to come as we are. We cannot save ourselves with Old Testament animal sacrifices. My prayer for you is that your spiritual eyes will be opened so that you can truly see that Jesus is the way, the truth, and the life, and that no one goes to the Father but through Him. Jesus is the gateway to the Father.

We have to see life's tragedies as win-win situations for those who are in Christ Jesus. Our bodies aren't meant to live forever. Ever since Adam sinned in the Garden of Eden, our bodies have gone back to the dust from which they came. We don't blame Adam for that, of course, although it's easy to think that if Adam had just obeyed God's one command, we wouldn't be in this situation. We cannot go back and change the past, but we can change the future.

If you don't want to see death, do what Elijah and Enoch did. They were consumed by thoughts of pleasing God. I'll admit that I would love to leave this world without tasting death, but I'm not consumed with thinking about God every second of the day. My thoughts are on the cares of this world and my family, as I pray that they will make wise decisions in life. You might be praying that your children won't go down the path of alcohol, drugs, and idolatry. You want your children to stay on the straight and narrow path and not deviate from it. But if your children are like the prodigal son, there is hope and light at the end of that tunnel. The prodigal son finally did come to his senses and wake up, and then he repented and was restored. So stop worrying about your children, and turn them over to the Father. Let go and let God orchestrate their lives, by repeating these words:

> Father, thank you for letting me be a steward over my children. Now I give them back to you. Their futures are in Your hands, as I trust You from this day forward. I choose this day to cast all my cares upon you, because I know that You care for me. You promised never to leave me or forsake me, and You are not a man that You should lie. I know that You have my best interests at heart. I know that I serve an awesome, epic, and loving God, and for that I worship and praise Your Holy name. In Jesus's name, amen!

So don't try to manipulate God by telling Him sad stories. Just trust Him.

The Bible tells us that God will keep us in perfect peace if our minds are fixed on Him. I do want peace in my life, instead of chaos. Religion will never set us free; in fact, it will keep us in bondage. Jesus came to set the captive free from religion, past hurts, sin, and the cares of this world. The church has to be built on the true foundation, which is Jesus Christ.

On January 14, 2018, I had a dream about someone who started to frame a house, but then discovered that the foundation was missing. Either the old foundation had been ripped out because it wasn't firm, or the man had started to build on someone else's foundation. However, the dream showed that he planned to rebuild the foundation, because he brought in new gravel.

We need to run back to our first love, the true foundation. We need Jesus now more than ever. That was the first thing I noticed. So I asked, in my dream, why they were framing without pouring the foundation first. Then I speculated that maybe they had dug up the old foundation and were going to replace it with the true foundation. (Read 1 Corinthians 3:11–12, Isaiah 28:16, Luke 14:29, and Romans 15:20.) Don't build on another man's foundation. (Read John 17:24, 1 Corinthians 3:10, 2 Timothy 2:19, and Hebrews 6:1.)

My dream revealed that there had been a foundation there at one time, but that the old foundation had to be laid again. The dream showed that the builder started framing without waiting for the new foundation to be poured. When I asked God about the meaning of this dream, He revealed to me that the dream showed that they were laying a foundation of repentance again. "Wherefore leaving the doctrine of the first principles of Christ, let us press on unto perfection; not laying again a foundation of repentance from dead works, and of faith toward God" (Hebrews 6:1 NKJV).

The church needs to build on the true foundation once and for all, and that true foundation is Jesus Christ. What foundation have you laid? A religious or legalistic foundation is not a true foundation, although the devil will try to trick you into thinking that it is, nor is a fleshly foundation a true foundation. Those foundations are nothing but dead works, and when one of life's storms hits, those foundations will not stand. God is trying to tear up those old foundations and rebuild the only true foundation, which is Jesus Christ. "And this will we do, if God permit. For as touching those who were once enlightened and tasted of the heavenly gift, and were made partakers of the Holy Spirit, and tasted the good word of God, and the powers of the age to come, and then fell away, it is impossible to renew them again unto repentance; seeing they crucify to themselves the Son of God afresh, and put him to an open shame" (Hebrews 6:3–6 ASV).

If the church continues to sleep in sin, it will also continue laying a foundation of repentance from dead works, over and over again. When we keep doing that, our hearts are hardened, making it impossible to be renewed again unto repentance. Jesus died once and for all for our sin, and He will not come back and do that again. Paying the price for our sin was a one-time deal. It's so easy to get entangled with sin if we don't keep walking in the Spirit.

Sometimes God gives us dreams in which He allows us to see people or things with which we are familiar. My mom, who died on January 24, 2013, was in this dream, and I caught a brief glimpse of my dad, who died on May 1, 1998.

When I prayed about this dream, God led me to Hebrews 6:1, which is about the foundation of repentance. satan tries to trick us into continuing down the path of unrighteousness and to entangle us in sins from many years ago. He wants us to keep tripping over those past sins, so that we cannot move on with God. Don't listen to satan and entertain those past sins again. Stop spinning your wheels by laying a foundation of repentance from dead works. Greater is He who is in us than he who is in the world. We are not defeated—we are victorious through Christ Jesus.

In 1998, after my father died, I had a dream in which someone came up with the idea of digging up my dad and going through the funeral process again. Why anyone would want to relive what is dead and buried? That's just like our past sins, which God has thrown into the sea of forgetfulness so that He won't remember them. If we listen to the devil, he will remind us over and over about our past sins. Since he continues to bring up our past, we should start reminding him of his future, when he will be thrown into the pit of hell for eternity. It was never intended for us to return to our vomit. When Jesus cleans our hearts and makes them His home, we should fill them with the Word of God.

Say this with me:

> Jesus, from this day forward, I choose to listen to your voice. I refuse to lay a foundation of repentance from dead works, because you died for my sins once and for all. I choose this day to live a victorious life, for satan is my defeated foe. I choose to live as an overcomer, because of the words of my testimony and the blood of the Lamb. I choose this day to walk in the Spirit, so that I'll no longer fulfill the lust of the flesh. satan, I'm tired of you reminding me of my past sins, and I refuse to return to my vomit. Instead, I'll live for the one who died on the cross

for my sin. Greater is He who is in me than he who lives in this world. I choose not to allow religion to dictate to me what I can and cannot do, and I bind legalism in Jesus's name. I choose to allow Jesus to be my peace and my rest. I know that religion is man's doing, but Christianity is God's doing through His Son, Jesus Christ. I know that religion could never be the gateway to heaven; Jesus is the only gateway to heaven and to the Father. I choose that straight and narrow path from this day forward, in Jesus's name.

God wants you to have a repentant heart, because the days in which we live are perilous and a dangerous culture. God wants us to shape the culture we live in one person at a time, starting with the person in the mirror.

~ FOURTEEN ~

The Peril of Falling Away

If I stay awake in Jesus, then my life is not my own. I have been bought with a price. The blood of Jesus paid for my life. But if I remain asleep, my life will be my own and I can selfishly do whatever I want. I can live precariously, coming and going as I please.

A child of God should remain sober and vigilant about the enemy. Today it's dangerous for a believer to live a careless life. If you go out to bars or lounges, the devil could use someone to spike your drink. If you think it's okay to do drugs, the devil will tell someone to give you some bad drugs. Going out to bars is dangerous because there are frequent shootings in bars.

After I was saved, I didn't live a victorious life. I was still living precariously—going to bars and sleeping in sin—and I could have easily been killed by satan. I wanted to have my cake and eat it too, because I forgot that my life was not my own. That was when I went into a deep depression. God wanted the prodigal child in me to wake up, but I was lulled by satan into a deep sleep. I was on a suicide mission with my life, but I didn't know it. The devil comes to kill, steal, and destroy, and I was at his beck and call. I didn't know much about the Holy Spirit, who wasn't prevalent in my life.

If you're heading down this path, I pray that you will wake up and immediately get back on the straight and narrow path. God loves you very much, and Jesus wants you to live a victorious life. Seek the face of God and flee from your precarious life. Jesus wants you to come back home, prodigal child. If you're not living under God's umbrella of protection, satan can have a field day with you.

In a conversation with the devil one day, God asked, "Have you considered my servant Job?" God told satan that he could do whatever he wanted to with Job except kill him. I remember being in a bar and asking God to leave me alone, because I wanted to live my life precariously. But God knew that satan had me under a deep sleep in sin and that I was battling depression. He knew that it wasn't really me, and I'm glad He didn't leave me.

Being depressed causes people to sleep around. When you're having sex with someone, you're tying your two souls together. That person could have a sexually transmitted disease or a demon, but you wouldn't know until it had been transferred to you. When you're living a precarious life, God is continuously telling you to wake up. He didn't plan for you to be soul tied to the devil. God doesn't want us in abusive relationship, but satan does. He wants you to be a defeated foe. He doesn't want us to be anything that God has called us to be. satan wants you to continue living a precarious, promiscuous life. The devil's goal is to kill you when he is finished using you.

Child of God, I implore you to snap out of your satan-induced trance and be set free in Jesus's name. When you have been delivered from satan's sleep-in-sin trap, then you must find someone else who has been lulled into that trap and help them wake up. It's going to be difficult talking about your past, but you persevered. You've weathered the storm, so now help someone else do the same. The devil wants to paralyze you with fear, doubt, intimidation, unforgiveness, depression, oppression, unbelief, doubt, worry, condemnation, sleep-in-sin walking, and hatred. But Jesus wants to liberate you from the devil's strong hold and spiritual assault on every aspect of your life, family, and ministry.

The devil rejoices when we keep silent about things that matter. When you're facing adversity, look it straight in the eye and rebuke it. God in you is greater than any adversity. Repent from your wicked ways and rebuke depression. I didn't know that I was in a deep sleep in sin, because I didn't know that the devil sent a spirit of depression. When you're facing depression, ask God to search your heart to see if you have any wicked ways of which you're unaware. Ask God to show you what doors you opened to invite that spirit of depression in. If there were word curses spoken over you, ask God to allow the Holy Spirit to break them and replace them with words of life. Word curses could have been spoken over your life by a family member, teacher, or other authority figure. Also, ask Him to reveal to you any time that you allowed sin into the camp. Job's situation was different, because he didn't sin. But the devil still tormented him, because God lifted His hedge of protection around Job.

The church should be undaunted when facing satan's fiery darts. The church should be bold and courageous, not fainthearted or cowardly. The church should mount up with wings as eagles. The church should not be envious of anyone or anything, especially the prosperity of the wicked.

FIFTEEN

Envious in the Heart

How will you know if you are still sleeping in sin? You will know because you'll be jealous of the prosperity of the wicked. Jealousy is an indicator that you have not yet awakened. The Bible clearly tells us not to be envious. "For I was envious of the arrogant when I saw the prosperity of the wicked" (Psalm 73:3). When you see self-centered, arrogant people living in ease and prosperity, envy will cunningly sneak into your heart. It's difficult when those evildoers speak with malice instead of compassion. They despise God and don't want to believe that He even exists, and yet we see them being successful and enjoying life. It seems like everything is going great for them, as though being evil protects them from evil, which is as ludicrous as it sounds. When the devil has finished using you like a puppet, he will kill you.

David struggled with envy, even though he was just as wealthy as the evildoers. The Bible tells us that David complained to God about how he was feeling. But God showed David that the riches and success of the wicked are fragile, like a dream, and could perish in a moment. "A good man leaves an inheritance to his children's children, but the sinner's wealth is laid up for the righteous" (Proverbs 13:22). Father, I receive this good news in Jesus's name. In the year 2018, I claim that the wicked's wealth will come swiftly to me. Wherever your treasure is, your heart will be too, and the hearts of the wicked are with their treasure. There is no need for God's people to envy wealthy people, because their wealth is stored up for the believers. If you receive that, then say, "Amen."

In the Old Testament, during the time of Abraham, Isaiah, and Jacob, God allowed Egypt to prosper. When God allows certain people to prosper, He always has a reason. Do you remember the story of Joseph being sold into slavery in Egypt by his brothers? He found favor with the Pharaoh. God will give you favor with man if you just walk with Him. "Little did Joseph's brothers know that selling him to a passing caravan was part of a divine orchestration of events, preparing their younger brother to be positioned to have authority over all the food supply in Egypt. Joseph, just one of many sons from an ordinary family, grew to be a man who, at an opportune time, saved his entire people from being wiped out by famine."[18] (Read Genesis 37:25–28 and chapters 42–46.)

Many scripture passages tell us not to be envious of other people. "Do not envy a man of violence and do not choose any of his ways" (Proverbs 3:31). Who in their right mind would envy a violent man? Only someone who is sleeping in sin would do that. Did you know that envy will rot your bones? "A tranquil heart gives life to the flesh, but envy makes the bones rot" (Proverbs 14:30). Is envy worth having your bones rot?

I have to stay on guard against being envious. At my workplace, I've discovered that some people engage in prostitution in exchange for promotions. Prostitution is the act of having sex in exchange for money, but it can also be viewed as exchanging your body for what you want, quid pro quo. We think of prostitution as a street worker's profession, but I'm here to tell you that prostitution exists in the workforce too. Some people look down on street prostitutes and judge them, but they don't look down on prostitutes in the workforce. Prostitution is prostitution, regardless of where you are selling your body. It's a sin, but you don't have to use your body that way any longer. Just repent before God and He will forgive you.

"Let not your heart envy sinners, but continue in the fear of the Lord all the day" (Proverbs 23:17). God wants us to wake up and submit to Him. He doesn't want us to continue in the sleep in sin by walking in the flesh.

How will you know that you are walking in the flesh? The Bible warns us about things such as envy, drunkenness, and orgies, so we need to take heed and shy away from them. "Now the works of the flesh are evident: sexual immorality, impurity, sensuality, idolatry, sorcery, enmity, strife, jealousy, fits of anger, rivalries, dissensions, divisions, envy, drunkenness, orgies, and things like these. I warn you, as I warned you before, that those who do such things will not inherit the kingdom of God" (Galatians 5:19–21 ESV).

Why would God mention both jealousy and envy, which have similar meanings? When that green-eyed monster raises its ugly head, you cannot contain it. You want be able to hear the voice of God when you become enraged with jealousy and envy. Merriam-Webster, Inc. dictionary on the Apple I-Tune App dated 2018 defines envy as the feeling of wanting to have what someone else has. Jealousy is an unhappy or angry feeling of wanting to have what someone else has. That's why you need to pray to God and ask Him to search your heart every day. "Search me, O God, and know my heart: try me, and know my thoughts: And see if there be any wicked way in me, and lead me in the way everlasting" (Psalm 139:23–24 KJV).

The Bible categorizes jealousy and envy as evil things. Envy will defile you, just like pride, murder, and adultery. We think of envy as a small sin, but God says that it is evil. "And He said, 'What comes out of a person is what defiles him. For from within, out of the heart of man, come evil thoughts, sexual immorality, theft, murder, adultery, coveting, wickedness, deceit, sensuality, envy, slander, pride, foolishness. All these evil things come from within, and they defile a person'" (Mark 7:22).

Church, it's time to awaken and keep our ways pure before the Lord. Envy and those other things that should not be mentioned among you make you unclean and unworthy. They will corrupt your perfection and make you immature. Envy violates you and separates you from God. As you know, it's easy to be envious today when so many people have big houses and fancy cars. That's why we need to wake up and turn our eyes back to Jesus. In Bible times, people rode camels and lived in tents, and it would probably be hard to really be jealous of someone else's camel—but easy to be envious of someone living in a palace.

The church needs to put away envy and other fleshly desires, which should have no place in our hearts. God wants us to awaken and put those evil things away. "So put away all malice and all deceit and hypocrisy and envy and all slander" (1 Peter 2:1). One of the devil's schemes is to set up a stronghold by persuading us to be envious and keep those things hidden. However, God wants us to be transparent so that those things can be exposed.

Pastors, please examine yourselves to see if you are preaching the Word of God with envy in your hearts. "Some indeed preach Christ from envy and rivalry, but others from good will" (Philippians 1:15). And pastors, don't compare your preaching with how another pastor preaches. God anointed you to preach in a unique style, and you don't have to preach with an eloquent tongue. If the Holy Spirit is in control and ordering your footsteps, then it's not you speaking anyway. You are just a vessel being used by the Holy Spirit. But if you're preaching in envy, then you have not awakened and you're being controlled by the enemy. "Preach the word; be ready in season and out of season; reprove, rebuke, and exhort, with complete patience and teaching" (2 Timothy 4:2).

Paul said that God did not call him to preach the gospel with words of eloquent wisdom. Sometimes we get so caught up in trying to use eloquent words that we water down the gospel. We want people to think that we are articulate and silver-tongued, but the blood of Jesus will never lose its power. Pastors, you don't have to use the pulpit to show off your ability to use language clearly and effectively. Paul said that's not necessary: "For Christ did not send me to baptize but to preach the gospel, and not with words of eloquent wisdom, lest the cross of Christ be emptied of its power" (1 Corinthians 1:17).

When the church has been awakened, we should be walking in love—not envy. "Love is patient and kind; love does not envy or boast; it is not arrogant" (1 Corinthians 13:4). We don't get to pick and choose who we show agape love to.

Why should you be envious of people who are blatantly walking in sin, which is contrary to the Word of God? "The sexual immoral, men who practice homosexuality, enslavers, liars, perjurers, and whatever else is contrary to sound doctrine" (1 Timothy 1:10). All these things are contrary to the Word of God, and He doesn't want His children to partake of such. Church, it's high time to wake up in Jesus's name. "For we ourselves were once foolish, disobedient, led astray, slaves to various passions and pleasures, passing our days in malice and envy, hated by others and hating one another" (Titus 3:3).

If you walk in love, you will not walk as a hater and a liar. The church is supposed to hate the sin but love the sinners.

 SIXTEEN

Haters and Liars

You are not awakening when you claim that you love God, but you hate your brother in Christ Jesus. Having hatred in your heart is like having cancer throughout your body. The Bible tells us that the heart is desperately wicked. Why continue to allow the devil to have a stronghold in this area of your life? Do you not realize that the devil hates you? But God knows your heart, and He sees the hatred you have for people who are different from you. "If anyone says, 'I love God,' and hates his brother, he is a liar; for he who does not love his brother whom he has seen cannot love God whom he has not seen" (1 John 4:20).

"You are of your father the devil, and your will is to do your father's desires. He was a murderer from the beginning, and does not stand in the truth, because there is no truth in him. When he lies, he speaks out of his own character, for he is a liar and the father of lies" (John 8:44). If you keep lying, you cannot be freed from the devil's strong hold. Why continue to fool yourself into thinking that you love God, but hate people who are different from you? Haters and liars go hand in hand. You are being deceived by the devil, so be awakened in Jesus's name.

If God calls you a hater and a liar, He's just calling it the way He sees it. It's not in God's nature to lie, nor will He contradict His Word. "By no means! Let God be true though everyone were a liar, as it is written, that you may be justified in your words, and prevail when you are judged" (Romans 3:4). "Whoever believes in the Son of God has the testimony in himself. Whoever does not believe God has made him a liar, because he has not believed in the testimony that God has borne concerning His Son" (1

John 5:10). I implore you in Jesus's name to stop listening to the deceitful voice of the devil. He was a murderer and liar from the beginning. It is the devil's nature to keep you from knowing the truth and to keep you in the dungeon of sleepiness.

Why does God hate liars? "There are six things that the Lord hates, seven that are an abomination to him: haughty eyes, a lying tongue, and hands that shed innocent blood, a heart that devises wicked plans, feet that make haste to run to evil, a false witness who breathes out lies, and one who sows discord among brothers" (Proverbs 6:16–19 ESV). You are doing these things because you are under the devil's sleep-in-sin spell. But that's not who you really are, so you need to awaken in Jesus's name.

The church will know it is no longer sleeping when we start showing agape love for one another and stop looking at the color of a person's skin. Red, yellow, black, and white are all precious in His sight. (Read John 3:16.) That's why God tells us to walk by faith and not by sight. We need to keep hatred, lying, adultery, fornication, idolatry, pride, lasciviousness, jealousy, wickedness, and greed under our feet. (Read Philippians 4:1–8.)

Church, when we start pondering and thinking about these things, then we will know that we are in a great awakening: "Finally, brothers, whatever is true, whatever is honorable, whatever is just, whatever is pure, whatever is lovely, whatever is commendable, if there is any excellence, if there is anything worthy of praise, think about these things" (Philippians 4:8). There will be praise coming from your lips, and the peace of God, which surpasses all understanding, will guard your hearts and your thoughts in Christ Jesus.

If the church meditates on the Word of God, you will not be prejudiced against your brothers and sisters in Christ or against nonbelievers.

~ SEVENTEEN ~

Prejudicial Ignorance/Brother Hater

How do we know that we are sleeping in sin? We know when we are walking in prejudicial ignorance. Why is there still hatred and bigotry among Christians? Why are we still separated and dividing the cross? Prejudicial ignorance is not bliss. Do you not know that God is the creator of us all? Red, yellow, black, and white are all precious in God's sight, and we all were created in His image, so we're beautiful creations.

Remember Moses's sister Miriam? She was one of God's prophetesses who had prejudicial ignorance toward Moses's wife, an Ethiopian woman. Numbers 12:1 says, "Then Miriam and Aaron spoke against Moses, because of the Ethiopian woman whom he had married." Miriam and Aaron thought that the Ethiopian woman's skin was inferior to their own. Did God see something wrong with Moses marrying outside his race? Of course not, because we were all created in God's Image. Man looks at the outside, at the color of a person's skin, but God looks inside at a person's heart, soul, and spirit.

Here's what God thinks about prejudice in our hearts: "So the anger of the Lord was aroused against them [Miriam and Aaron], and He departed. And when the cloud departed from above the tabernacle, suddenly Miriam became leprous, as white as snow. Then Aaron turned toward Miriam, and there she was a leper. So, Aaron said to Moses, 'Oh, my Lord! Please do not lay this sin on us, in which we have done foolishly and in which we have sinned'" (Numbers 12:9). The price of prejudicial ignorance is high. Miriam was a prophetess and Aaron was a priest, so they both held high positions over God's people and should have known better. But when we're lulled into satan's deep-sleep trap, our minds become cloudy.

Why did God curse only Miriam with leprosy? Well, as a priest, Aaron had to go into the tabernacle's holy of holies on behalf of the people, and nothing unclean could enter into the Holy of Holies. Could someone be in a high position within the church today and still have prejudice or hatred in their heart? Psalm 139:23 says, "Search me, O God, and know my heart; try me, and know my thoughts: And see if there be any wicked way in me, and lead me in the way everlasting."

Jeremiah 17:9 says, "The heart is deceitful above all things and desperately wicked: who can know it?" Only God knows it. Man cannot know another person's heart. As Christians, we need to set our faces like flint before the Lord so we can be separated from unholy worldly influences. God loves the sinner but hates the sin. David stayed on his face before the Lord constantly, because he knew how the flesh was capable of sinning. When you have prejudice in your heart, God always has the solution. Second Chronicles 7:14 says, "If My people who are called by My name will humble themselves, and pray and seek My face, and turn from their wicked ways, then I will hear from heaven, and will forgive their sin and heal their land."

God is calling us individually and corporately as a body of believers to fall before Him on our faces. Then the Holy Spirit will set us free from prejudicial ignorance and snatch us from the enemy's sleep-in-sin lair. God wants to forgive our sin so that our land can be healed, but we have to allow Him to do that. Give God full carte blanche over your life. The Holy Spirit will not force Himself on anyone. If you want to hold on to your prejudicial spirit, don't expect forgiveness for your sins or healing for your land. If you think it's okay to hold on to those things in your heart, then you are behaving like a hypocrite.

The Southern Baptist Convention separated from the Baptist Convention because of prejudice. Southern Baptists allowed the enemy to make them believe that a black person did not have a soul. That's how cunning satan is. In 1995, the Southern Baptist Convention denounced racism as a deplorable sin and apologized to African-Americans for the sin of slavery. Then they asked forgiveness from their black brothers and sisters for the individual and systemic form of racism that still exists in our churches and society even today. Baptists in Atlanta on that day affirmed that every human life is sacred and vowed to pursue racial reconciliation.

I once heard someone say that we are divided on Sundays. We have black churches, white churches, Hispanic churches, Asian churches, and so on. If we truly want a great revival to break out in our land, then we need to come together as one body in Christ Jesus and cut out all this foolishness. We need to demonstrate to the world that the church wants reconciliation. Yes, they will know that we are Christians by our love—our love for one another, and our love for them. If we say that we love God but hate our brother, we are being hypocrites. It is impossible for us to win this world for Christ when we holding on to prejudice and hatred in our hearts.

Some churches allow a few blacks and people of other races to worship with them, but they will not invite them over for dinner at their homes. If you shun people, you have prejudice in your heart. There is a way that seems right to man, but leads to destruction. Holding on to ignorant prejudice will lead you to destruction. God looks at the heart, and man looks at the outer appearance. We are behaving vainly when we think one race is superior to another.

Can Christians live in peace and harmony with one another? Can we break down these prejudicial barriers? Yes, we can, but it's a choice that we have to make every single day. Do we walk in prejudicial ignorance today, or do we walk like Christ Jesus? We must wake up to satan's devices. He wants us to stay in a trance so we won't be effective for this world. If you have prejudicial ignorance in your heart, you need to confess it. I believe the Holy Spirit is convicting you right now to let it all go. Please be obedient and repent; don't listen to the enemy or your flesh any longer. Jesus is telling us to come to the light, where there is no darkness, prejudice, or sin.

"Whoever says he is in the light and hates his brother is still in darkness. Whoever loves his brother abides in the light, and in him there is no cause for stumbling. But whoever hates his brother is in the darkness and walks in the darkness, and does not know where he is going, because the darkness has blinded his eyes" (1 John 2:9–11 ESV). If you thinking you are walking in the light, but you hate your brother, then you are sleeping in sin. How can you say that you love God but hate your brother? The enemy, who hates you, has tricked you. He wants you to remain asleep in Sin Dungeon so that he can continue to torture you.

God is love and love is God, no matter how you slice it. God, who will never change, tells us in His Word to be holy in our conduct. If the church continues to walk in darkness, we will betray Jesus, but that's not who we are. We aren't the devil's children—we are children of the most high God.

EIGHTEEN

Betraying Jesus

When the enemy has lulled you into the sleep in sin, it will cause you to betray Jesus like Judas Iscariot did. Whenever you clothe yourself with a religious spirit, it will cause you to betray Jesus. To betray means to hurt someone who trusts you, such as a friend or relative, by not helping them or by doing something morally wrong. When Judas Iscariot opened the door for the devil to use him during the Last Supper, Jesus knew that the devil had come upon Judas. Jesus told Judas to go and do whatever he needed to do. While Jesus and His disciples were in the garden of Gethsemane, Judas and a group of soldiers showed up to arrest Him. For thirty pieces of silver, Judas betrayed Jesus with a kiss. Greed will cause you to do things that you'd never imagine—illegal and evil things.

How are you betraying Jesus? Are you doing things that are morally wrong and willfully sinning? Are you prostituting the Word of God? I had never seen Jesus betrayed in this way until the Holy Spirit revealed it to me. When a Christian lives in habitual sin, they are betraying Jesus. When you wall in your anger, you are betraying Jesus. In John 18:10, while Peter was in the garden of Gethsemane, he angrily drew his sword and cut off the ear of the high priest's servant, and Jesus had to heal it.

Being consumed by anger will cause you to cut someone's ear off, just like Peter did. He was under the impression that he was protecting Jesus, but the Word of God says that if you live by the sword, you will die by the sword. Jesus doesn't need for us to defend Him, since He could have easily summoned legions of angels to protect Him. But He knew that wasn't the Father's will, and everything Jesus did was based on pleasing the Father. If you want to please the Father like Jesus did, then remember that obedience is better than sacrifice.

When the enemy is finished with you, he will cause a great sense of guilt and condemnation to fall upon you. He will tempt you and put thoughts of suicide in your head, like he did with Judas Iscariot. That's how the devil operates—he'll torment you until you break. The only thing Judas had to do was to repent. Jesus knew that Judas was being used by the devil, and Judas would have been forgiven if he had repented. Jesus wasn't surprised when Judas betrayed Him, and He stayed focused on His mission. Jesus came to die for our sin, and nothing was going to keep Him from fulfilling that great mission. Jesus was all about the Father's business. When you betray Jesus, just repent and turn from your wicked ways, and He will forgive you. Repentance is one of the keys to restoration with the Father.

After Adam and Eve sinned in the garden of Eden, all they had to do was repent. If they had asked God for forgiveness, He would have forgiven them. But don't let pride set in, because if you keep listening to the voice of the enemy, who came to kill, steal, and destroy, you'll never think about repenting. God wants you to stop going down the path of unrighteousness and start silencing the voice of the enemy, so that you won't sleep in Sin Dungeon any longer. Remember that suicide is not the way to escape condemnation; repentance is the only path to forgiveness. When you contemplate suicide, you are playing into the devil's hands. You need to tell the devil to shut up and go away, in Jesus's name. If you really mean it, then just watch that sucker flee from you.

I pray that you will see yourself the way God sees you—not the way the devil sees you. The devil hates you and wants you dead, and he'll try his hardest to keep you from living a victorious life. The devil doesn't want to see you as a conqueror, but as a defeated foe. As the Bible tells us in Jeremiah, "I chose you before I formed you in the womb; I set you apart before you were born. I appointed you a prophet to the nations" (Jeremiah 1:5 HCSB). God's hand has always been upon you. You just have to believe and trust in Him.

The devil will always tell you that you're worthless, but God will tell you that you are worth everything to Him. That's why He sent His son to die on a cross for you. God created you in His image and you are precious to Him—unique and one of a kind. After God created you, He broke the mold to ensure that there will never be a duplicate of you. God has plans for you—a future and a hope in Jesus Christ. He wants you to prosper and be in good health, even as your soul prospers. When Jesus died for you, He said that He would go and prepare a place just for you in heaven. Jesus said that in His father's house are many mansions, and one of those mansions has your name on it. Just continue to fight the fight and keep the faith by being awakened. God loves you so much, and I pray that you will receive His love and start seeing yourself as being fearfully and wonderfully made. In God's eye, you are remarkable and awesome. God loves the sinner, but He has nothing but abhorrence for the sin.

It's okay to get angry, but it's a sin to *stay* angry. Ephesians 4:26 says, "Be you angry, and sin not; let not the sun go down upon your wrath; neither give place to the devil." When someone bullies you at school, cause a scene to get a teacher or other adult's attention. That's an act of strength and character. If you're in the restroom, where a lot of bullying occurs, scream as loud as you can to let the bullies know that their behavior is unwelcome. Bullies usually attack in groups, so never take matters into your own hands. Let an adult handle it. Bullying is an act of cowardice.

Stop grieving the Holy Spirit, which is another form of betraying Jesus. Remember that you are sealed for the day of redemption. Put away all bitterness, wrath, anger, clamor, and railing with all malice. Continue being kind one to another, tenderhearted and forgiving, because God in Christ forgave you. (Read Ephesians 4:26–32.)

When you let the sun go down on your wrath, you're giving the devil a stronghold in your life. Again, it's okay to get angry, but don't sin. Just leave your anger, wrath, bitterness, and unforgiveness at the foot of the cross. Cast your cares upon Jesus and tell Him how you feel about the situation. He will sympathize with you and go to bat for you. If someone is bullying you at school or on social media, just let God, your vindicator, take care of it. Allow these things to roll off you like water on a duck's back. God wants us to pursue peace, not revenge, because vengeance is His.

The name of Jesus is above every name. His name is above suicidal thoughts, bullying, cancer, pornography, greed, lasciviousness, gossiping, drug addiction, alcohol addiction, and so on. So whatever you are struggling with, replace it with the name of Jesus. (Read Philippians 2:8–11.)

"And being found in appearance as a man, He humbled Himself and became obedient to the point of death, even the death of the cross. There God also has highly exalted Him and given Him the name which is above every name, that at the name of Jesus every knee should bow, of those in heaven, and of those on earth, and of those under the earth, and that every tongue should confess that Jesus Christ is Lord, to the glory of God the Father" (Philippians 2:8–11 NKJV). Since Jesus's name is above every name, every knee will bow in heaven, on earth, and in hell.

I pray that you will come to understand this while you still have breath in you. All you have to do is confess that Jesus is Lord over your life—your circumstances, trials and tribulations, drug and pornography addictions, lasciviousness and greed, cancer, and all sickness and diseases. He can heal you and set you free from sickness and disease, if you'll just line your faith up with His. I pray that you won't make your bed in hell, forever separated from the God who created you in His image. This same God called you to a royal priesthood, and He is coming back for you soon. (Read 1 Thessalonians 4:16–18.)

You must confess with your mouth that you shall live and not die, and continue to repeat it until you truly believe it. The enemy is trying to hinder you from becoming what God has called you to become, which is a mighty person of valor. satan attacks those who don't know that they have a strong anointing on their lives, which is why he keeps telling you lies: that you're a drug addict, a pervert, a prostitute, a thief, and a liar, and that you'll never amount to anything. However, God sees you as worthy, and that's why He came to die for you. You are an overcomer by the blood of the lamb and the words of your testimony. You are not a drug addict, pervert, thief, or liar. Those are the devil's attributes, not yours.

You will become everything that God has called you to be. You are not a failure or a mistake, and God will never see you that way. It's up to you—believe God's truth, or continue to believe the lies of the devil. God gave you a free will, so the choice is yours. The devil is the prince of lies, but you are a child of the one and only true living God. You are not a defeated foe, because you have the victory in Christ Jesus.

The battle that you are going through is all in your mind. The devil is telling you to follow him down the path of destruction and damnation. But God wants you to take on the mind of Christ, so that you'll know how to silence the voice of the enemy. The Father has given you abundant life, and all you have to do is receive it. God wants to set you free from bondage and the cares of this world. That's why He sent His Son, to set the captive free from the lies of the enemy.

The flesh is weak but the spirit is strong. You will always have to battle your flesh if you don't keep it nailed on the cross. Your flesh will always tell you to give in to the devil's cunning little schemes. The devil will keep telling you to continue on the path of destruction and that you're not actually hurting your flesh by pleasing it. However, you need to tell the devil to get back under your feet. If you keep your foot pressed firmly against the devil's neck, you'll keep him silent and he won't be able to keep telling you those lies. The devil wants you to stay stuck, rather than moving forward with God.

More than two years ago, procrastination kept me from writing this book. The devil knows that this book is going to help someone become free in Jesus's name. God knows our hearts, and He knows that some of us just won't read His Word. So He inspires His people to write books like this to encourage us, let us know that we're beloved, and remind us of His plans for us.

God wants to give you a hope and a dynamic future, so He put me in time-out just like He did with Jonah. God put Jonah in the belly of a whale for three days just to get his attention. Obedience is better than sacrifice; it's better to obey God immediately than to procrastinate. The enemy kept telling me that nobody wanted to hear what I had to say, and he was right. But people *do* want to hear what God has to say, because it's the Word of God—not my words—that frees people from bondage. The real power is in the Word of God—not in my words.

The devil kept throwing guilt and condemnation at me, but I pray that everyone who reads this book will be set free once and for all from his snares. I pray that you will awaken in Jesus's name, that you'll mount up on wings like eagles, that you'll run the race set before you with endurance, and that you will not grow weary of doing good in Jesus's name. I pray that the devil will no longer hinder you from becoming a mighty man or woman of God. I pray that you will have such boldness for Jesus Christ in your life that the demons will tremble. I pray that you will have such strong faith in Jesus Christ that you can tell a mountain to move into the sea and it shall be done. I pray that you'll have a passion for winning souls for Jesus Christ and a strong love for your brothers and sisters in Christ Jesus. I pray that your faith will be so strong that it lacks nothing. I pray that your face will glow because you asked God to show you His glory. I pray that you will have an anointing on your life to draw men and women to Christ. This will be your great awakening.

"So then, we must not sleep, like the rest, but we must stay awake and be serious" (1 Thessalonians 5:6 HCSB). God takes your awakening seriously, and so should you. The devil wants you to remain asleep and paralyzed in Sin Dungeon, so that you won't be effective for Christ and the kingdom of God. But God wants you to be sober and "put on the breastplate of faith and love; and for a helmet, the hope of salvation" (1 Thessalonians 5:8). That's why God said in 1 Thessalonians 5:7, "For they that sleep, sleep in the night."

"Who died for us, so that whether we are awake or asleep, we will live together with Him. Therefore encourage one another and build each other up as you are already doing" (1 Thessalonians 5:10–11 HCSB). God doesn't want any of us to perish, so we need to awaken in Jesus's name. God wants you to abstain from every form of evil, but the devil, of course, does not. The devil wants you to remain asleep in sin so that he can control you, but God wants you to wake up and be free in Christ Jesus. We are day people like God—not night people like the devil. So continue to walk in the light, because the light of Jesus is in you.

I strongly believe that we are in the last days. Second Timothy 3:1–5 says, "That in the last days perilous times will come: For men will be lovers of themselves, lovers of money, boasters, proud, blasphemers, disobedient to parents, unthankful, unholy, unloving, unforgiving, slanderers, without self-control, brutal, despisers of good, traitors, headstrong, haughty, lovers of pleasure rather than lovers of God, having a form of godliness but denying its power. And from such people turn away!" In other words, stay as far away as possible from those people.

If you are asleep in sin, you will be lured into the trap that the devil has set for you, continuing to fulfill the lust of the flesh, lust of the eyes, and a prideful life. The devil wants to corrupt your mind, like the minds of people during the days of Sodom and Gomorrah. He wants you to remain in captivity so that you'll continue to do his will. If you continue to sleep in sin, you'll move deeper and deeper into darkness until it seems like there is no escape. "Evil people and impostors will become worse, deceiving and being deceived. But as for you, continue in what you have learned and firmly believed" (1 Timothy 3:13 HCSB). The devil wants you to continue to live a self-indulgent life, "But she that liveth in pleasure is dead while she liveth" (1 Timothy 5:6 KJV). But I'm here to tell you that it's not too late to break free from the sleep in sin. You can snap out of it and come to your senses, in Jesus's name.

God will bring back to your remembrance the sacred scriptures that you learned in childhood. "You know those who taught you, and you know that from childhood you have known the sacred Scriptures, which are able to give you wisdom for salvation through faith in Christ Jesus. All Scripture is inspired by God and is profitable for teaching, for rebuking, for correcting, for training in righteousness, so that the man of God may be complete, equipped for every good work" (1 Timothy 3:14–16 HCSB). "But as for you, continue in what you have learned and have firmly believed, knowing from whom you learned it and how from childhood you have been acquainted with the sacred writings, which are able to make you wise for salvation through faith in Christ Jesus. All Scripture is breathed out by God and profitable for teaching, for reproof, for correction, and for training in righteousness, that the man of God may be complete, equipped for every good work" (2 Timothy 3:14–17 ESV).

Demonic influence! "Now the Spirit explicitly says that in later times some will depart from the faith, paying attention to deceitful spirits and the teachings of demons, through the hypocrisy of liars whose consciences are seared. They forbid marriage and demand abstinence from foods that God created to be received with gratitude by those who believe and know the truth. For everything created by God is good, and nothing should be rejected if it is received with thanksgiving, since it is sanctified by the word of God and by prayer" (1 Timothy 4:1–5 HCSB). They probably forbid marriage because they witness so many divorces in the church.

"And that they may come to their senses and escape the snare of the devil, having been taken captive by him to do his will" (2 Timothy 2:26 NKJV). Once you have been set free from the devil's sleep in sin, you should repent and ask for God's forgiveness. We need to use the gift of repentance frequently.

106

~ NINETEEN ~

Divorces in the Church

How do we know that the church has been lulled into a deep sleep in Sin Dungeon? Because the church's divorce rate is just as high as the divorce rate in the broader world. God's Word tells us, "Do not be unequally yoked with unbelievers. For what partnership has righteousness with lawlessness? Or what fellowship has light with darkness?" (2 Corinthians 6:14 ESV).

Merriam-Webster, Inc. dictionary on the Apple I-Tune App dated 2018 defines a *yoke* as a bar or frame that is attached to the heads or necks of two work animals, such as oxen, so that they can pull a plow or heavy load. The yoke steers the animals in the direction that the person controlling it wants them to go. *Interpreting the Symbols and Types*, by Kevin Connor, describes *yoke* as a symbol of servitude, slavery, or fellowship.[19]

"For what partnership has righteousness with lawlessness? Or what fellowship has light with darkness? What accord has Christ with Belial? Or what portion does a believer share with an unbeliever?" (2 Corinthians 6:14–15). We can be unequally yoked not only in marriage, but in every aspect of our lives. Marriage is just one way to be unequally yoked. Some of us think that after we marry, we'll help our partner change. But we can't even change ourselves, so how can we change someone else? When we think this way, we're playing God, but we're supposed to plant the seeds and let the Holy Spirit do the watering. If God doesn't get hold of their heart, then we shouldn't marry them. We are not wiser than God, who is omniscient and knows our future. So let's trust God instead of our feelings, which can deceive us.

Now, if someone pretends to be a Christian, you'd better look at the kind of fruit they are producing. If they are producing the fruit of the Spirit, then by all means marry that person. "But the fruit of the Spirit is love, joy, peace, patience, kindness, goodness, faithfulness, gentleness, and self-control; against such things there is no law" (Galatians 5:22). If the person is walking in the Spirit and has crucified their flesh with its passions and desires, then they have been awakened and belong to Christ Jesus. We're all human, so sometimes we wake up on the wrong side of the bed or have a bad hair day, but that's just life.

God said that He will grant a divorce only if a wife or husband commits adultery, which means that they haven't awakened. "It was also said, Whoever divorces his wife, let him give her a certificate of divorce. But I say to you that everyone who divorces his wife, except on the ground of sexual immorality, makes her commit adultery, and whoever marries a divorced woman commits adultery" (Matthew 5:31–32 ESV). This scripture goes both ways, so let's be real. It's usually the husband who commits adultery. Many men have a wandering eye, especially when they're going through a midlife crisis.

> And Pharisees came up to Him and tested Him by asking, Is it lawful to divorce one's wife for any cause? He answered, Have you not read that He who created them from the beginning made them male and female, and said, Therefore a man shall leave his father and his mother and hold fast to his wife, and the two shall become one flesh? So they are no longer two but one flesh. What therefore God has joined together, let not man separate. They said to him, why then did Moses command one to give a certificate of divorce and to send her away? He said to them, Because of your hardness of heart, Moses allowed you to divorce your wives, but from the beginning it was not so. And I say to you: whoever divorces his wife, except for sexual immorality, and marries another, commits adultery. (Matthew 19:3–9)

~ TWENTY ~

Tipping and Robbing God

How do you know if you are walking in the sleep in sin? When you think that it's okay to tip God. If you aren't paying your tithes and offering to the Lord, you are walking in the sleep in sin. The enemy does not want you to realize this; he wants you to keep treating God like a waiter by offering Him a tip. Why does the sleeping church want to tip God or steal from Him? Because the devil has lulled us into the sleep in sin. "Will man rob God? Yet you are robbing me. But you say, 'How have we robbed you?' In your tithes and contributions" (Malachi 3:8 ESV).

Some people don't realize that they are robbing God. If you rob God, however, you will be cursed, so if things aren't going your way, you need to examine yourself. If you're frequently in and out of the doctor's office, is it because you're robbing God? Do you know that only 10 percent of churchgoers tithe? That is sad. God owns it all. We are just stewards over what He has entrusted us with. I'm not a pastor of a church, but I studied the book of Malachi several years ago. After that, I told myself that I didn't want to be cursed, so I can't afford *not* to give my tithe and offerings to my home church. "You are cursed with a curse, for you are robbing me, the whole nation of you" (Malachi 3:9 ESV).

Examine yourself, especially if your kids have gone astray from the Lord, to see if you are robbing God of His tithes and offerings. God wants us to bring the full tithe into the storehouse so that there will be food in His house. When a pastor wins souls, that requires money. God doesn't want us to be cursed. If you give your minimum of 10 percent and an offering, watch God open heaven's windows and pour down a blessing until there is no more need. God is not a man, so He won't lie to you, but I challenge you to give God what is rightfully His anyway and watch the blessings fall down.

"I will rebuke the devourer for you, so that it will not destroy the fruits of your soil, and your vine in the field shall not fail to bear, says the Lord of hosts. Then all nations will call you blessed, for you will be a land of delight, says the Lord of hosts" (Malachi 3:11–12 ESV). God wants us to prosper and be in good health, even as our souls prosper. God doesn't want the devil continually knocking at our door to devour our health, family, and job. To *devour* means to eat up greedily or ravenously, or to prey upon. Do you want the locusts to come in and devour the crops planted in your fields and everything you own? If not, then you need to awaken and start giving your tithes and offerings.

Why do we enjoy robbing God? The devil wants you to think that your money is yours and only yours, because you earned it. He wants to control you through greed, so he tells you that you're entitled to spend your money however you want to.

As a young teenager, I wasn't taught that everything belongs to God. Nobody taught me to pay my tithes and offering. Parents, if you have young kids, please teach them the principle of giving. Let them see how important it is to give God 10 percent of what He has blessed them with. If you give them an allowance, tell them to give 10 percent of it to God. If you teach them to give at an early age, it will become an ingrained habit and when they grow older, they'll continue to give 10 percent back to God.

If this concept is programmed into their brains, they are less likely to be greedy. Their obedience at a young age unties God's hands to rebuke the devourer for their sake. When they become adults, giving will be second nature for them. When you invest in the kingdom of God, you please God—not man. God does not want us to be ignorant when it comes to investing in His kingdom. We have to keep our giving in perspective and keep telling ourselves that it all belongs to God.

We need to realize that we are simply stewards of that which God has entrusted to us. I'm a living witness that the more money you earn, the more difficult it is to give your tithe and offering. It's so easy for greed to set in and tell you to buy this or that, and then you end up in debt. Soon the devil tells you that getting out of debt is more important than paying your tithe. It was the devil and your flesh that got you into debt in the first place.

That's what happened to me. I wanted a new car and the latest electronics gadgets, but I soon found myself in debt way over my head. God doesn't want us to live like that. He wants us to be awakened and live free from the slavery of debt. "Owe no man anything, but to love one another: for he that loveth another hath fulfilled the law" (Romans 13:8 KJV). If you're in a lot of debt, then the rich rule over you—and that is not God's plan for your life. "The rich rules over the poor, and the borrower is the slave of the lender" (Proverbs 22:7 ESV). God is calling His people out of debt, so that we can have an effect on this world. Debt will keep you in bondage.

My wife and I were on the road to getting out of debt, but then we had several accidents. We ended up buying two new cars within a year, so now we're working on getting out of debt again. We had told ourselves that we would never again have two car payments at the same time—and now we have two car payments. Several years ago, God told my wife and me to get out of debt, but then I fell under the devil's sleep-in-sin spell. God calls us to live a debt-free life. These aren't my words—they're the Word of God. I'm just the messenger, and I have to be obedient to God.

You should be like the widow who put all that she had into the offering basket. That widow understood the concept of stewardship. "And a poor widow came and dropped in two tiny coins worth very little" (Mark 12:41 ESV). By giving everything she had, she got Jesus's attention. If you want to get Jesus's attention, start giving unselfishly. Listen to what Jesus said about the widow who gave all she had: "Summoning His disciples, He said to them, 'I assure you: This poor widow has put in more than all those giving to the temple treasury. For they all gave out of their surplus, but she out of her poverty has put in everything she possessed—all she had to live on'" (Mark 12:43 ESV).

There have been many debates over whether we should tithe our gross income or our net income. If you give God His tithe and offering from the gross, you're giving Him your first fruits, before taxes, savings, and so on. If you pay your tithe and offering from your net income, however, you are giving God your leftovers, like Cain did. When you tithe your net income, you're giving to the government first and then giving God 10 percent of what is left, so your priorities are messed up. Are you robbing God? Yes, you are. I pray that God will reveal to you the error of your ways, so that every curse will be broken.

If you start giving unselfishly and obey the principle of giving, God will outgive you. "Give, and it will be given to you. Good measure, pressed down, shaken together, running over, will be put into your lap. For with the measure you use it will be measured back to you" (Luke 6:38 ESV). I don't give just to get something back from God. I give my tithes and offerings because He commands me to do so. If you give unselfishly, you are trusting God. Also, giving will hold back the devourer. You won't be giving all your money to doctors, pharmaceutical companies, and so on.

God wants to open the windows of heaven and shower you with blessings. He wants to remove any word and generational curses from you and your family. I pray that you will choose today to stop tipping God and giving Him your leftovers. I break the spirit of Cain off your life right now, in Jesus's name. I pray that you will trust God and give Him what is rightfully His.

I don't know about you, but I want nations to see that I'm blessed and highly favored by God. Then they, too, will want to be blessed, which creates a great opportunity to share your testimony about Jesus. You can tell them how He ended the devourer's curse on your life when you chose to give back to God what is rightfully His anyway. Tell them that you are just a steward over what He has entrusted you with. Tell them that if they'll trust Him with their tithes and offerings, God will rebuke the devourer for their sakes too, but they'll have to trust Him. When God can trust us with little things such as money, then He will be able to trust us with the bigger things.

Several years ago, God laid on my heart to start giving 15 percent instead of 10 percent. I was obedient, and my wife and I received so many blessings from that one act of obedience. I was truly living Luke 6:38. God does not want His people to live in poverty or barely make ends meet. Abraham, Isaac, and Jacob were blessed beyond measure because they understood stewardship. If you want the same blessings that Abraham received, then be obedient and give God His rightful tithes and offerings. And if God lays on your heart to give more than 10 percent, just do it; He wouldn't ask you to do that for no reason. I want to see you free from curses and the devourer, I want the nations to see that I am blessed and highly favored by God, and I want Jesus to get all the glory.

As you know, Abraham was counted as righteous because he obeyed and believed God. Abraham gave back to God what was rightfully His. I want my blessings to be pressed down, shaken together, and running over. What about you? If you know someone who is blessed beyond measure, ask them their secret. Also, remember that blessings don't have to come in the form of material things. Good health, living to a ripe old age, and seeing your grandchildren are also blessings. Job saw four generations and counted that as a blessing.

Jesus understood the principle of stewardship. He knew that His life wasn't His own, and He made the ultimate sacrifice by giving back to God what was rightfully God's. Jesus knew that God created man and woman in His image, so we belong to Him. Jesus laid down His life and offered it back to God. Our lives are not our own, because we have been bought with a price. I believe Jesus said to the Father, "I have made the ultimate sacrifice for your people, and I present to You the blood for every one of their past, present, and future sins." Jesus held up His end of the bargain, and now it's up to us to believe and receive what Jesus did on the cross. Jesus gave His life willingly for our sakes, and He offers salvation and forgiveness for our sins.

God doesn't want anyone to perish and be separated from Him, and that's why He sent Jesus, His only son. "For God so loved the world that He gave His only begotten Son, that whosoever believes on Him should not perish, but have eternal life" (John 3:16). Jesus is telling you that you are worthy, so now all you have to do is believe Him. Stop listening to the lies of the devil, who will tell you that you are unworthy. God doesn't require you to do what Jesus has already done to pay for your sins. God knows that we are fully human, and Jesus was both fully divine and fully human. Since we were created as human beings, Jesus had to come to earth in the form of a man, thus demonstrating the power of true agape love.

The late Dr. Martin Luther King Jr. once said, "We must discover the power of love, the redemptive power of love. And when we do that, we will make of this old world a new world, for love is the only way." The nature of this type of love should have already been revealed to the church of all people. This is the love that God demonstrated when He sent His son to die on a cross over two thousand years ago. This love covers a multitude of sins. This is the kind of love in which the church should be walking every day. This love goes beyond the color of a person's skin or the bondage and sin in which a person might be trapped. The church is supposed to hate the sin but love the sinner. Jesus showed the power of love on the cross, presenting His body as a living sacrifice, and then He rose from the dead.

God has given us gifts and abilities, not so that we can compete with one another, but so that we can be a blessing and an encouragement to others. Don't be weighed down by a plethora of problems, regardless if they are big or small, but turn them over to Jesus. He said to cast all of our cares upon Him, because He cares for us.

Church, if you want to be a blessing to others, don't commit sacrilege by giving God your leftovers. God wants your first fruit.

TWENTY-ONE

Leftover Offering

How do I know the church is sleeping? I know because we bring to God's storehouse our leftovers:

> In the course of time Cain brought to the Lord an offering of the fruit of the ground, and Abel also brought of the firstborn of his flock and of their fat portions. And the Lord had regard for Abel and his offering, but for Cain and his offering he had no regard. So Cain was very angry, and his face fell. The Lord said to Cain, "Why are you angry, and why has your face fallen? If you do well, will you not be accepted? And if you do not do well, sin is crouching at the door. Its desire is contrary to you, but you must rule over it." (Genesis 1:3–7)

Cain presented God with blemished fruit of the ground, whereas Abel brought the firstborn of his flock. Abel knew how to please God, but Cain didn't even care about pleasing God. God gave Cain another chance to make it right, but his heart was hardened.

Cain got angry because he wanted God to accept his leftovers. How can we, as the body of Christ, present the creator of the world with leftovers? God created us in His image. He knows that when we don't do the right thing, sin will be crouching at the door ready to pounce on us. We give God our leftovers because we have been lulled into the enemy's sleep in Sin Dungeon. God tells us that we must rule over it by doing the right thing. "By faith Abel offered to God a more acceptable sacrifice than Cain, through which he was commended as righteous, God commending him by accepting his gifts. And through his faith, though he died, he still speaks" (Hebrews 11:4).

When we give God our best, it will be commended to us as righteous. "Will man rob God? Yet you are robbing Me. But you say, 'How have we robbed You?' In your tithes and contributions. You are cursed with a curse, for you are robbing Me, the whole nation of you" (Malachi 3:8–9). Church, if you don't want to remain cursed, then wake up and bring God His full tithe and offering so that there may be food in His house. God told us to put Him to the test and then watch what He will do for us. "'Bring the full tithe into the storehouse, that there may be food in My house. And thereby put me to the test,' says the Lord of hosts, 'if I will not open the windows of heaven for you and pour down for you a blessing until there is no more need. I will rebuke the devourer for you, so that it will not destroy the fruits of your soil, and your vine in the field shall not fail to bear,' says the Lord of hosts" (Malachi 3:10–11).

So the excellent sacrifice to make is to give your full offering to God. Is an offering of 5 percent an acceptable sacrifice? Of course not. God requires us to give at least 10 percent of our gross income, which is our first fruit. One reason why I give my tithe and offering to the Lord is that I don't want to be cursed. Why anyone would want to be cursed is beyond me. When we rob God, we give the devil ammunition to keep us trapped like a rat. So keep your eyes looking toward God, for He will rescue you from the enemy's traps. "My eyes are ever toward the Lord, for he will pluck my feet out of the net" (Psalm 25:15 ESV).

According to Robert Stearns, "In light of this, consider America where according to Barna's research, less than 10 percent of Christians who attend church give a tithe of their income (10 percent or more) to churches or other Christian organizations. This amounts to millions of dollars every year that is held back from much needed use in God's Kingdom."[20] The reason why this is happening is that the church is sleeping in sin. We need a great spiritual awakening.

"Vindicate me, O Lord, for I have walked in my integrity, and I have trusted in the Lord without wavering. Prove me, O Lord, and try me; test my heart and my mind" (Psalm 26:1). Do you really trust God in your tithe and offering?

Have you ever wondered what's going on with my children? Look at you, giving to see if it lines up with the Word of God. According to Robert Stearns, the church is losing its young people because we lack a moral compass. We have lowered the standard of what it means to be a Christian. We have become a people without a moral compass, in most respects no different from unbelievers. After proclaiming that our faith is no better than any other, our young people seem to be taking our words at face value and leaving the church in droves.[21] Why are young people leaving the church? Because the enemy has lowered them into the sleep in Sin Dungeon; they're trapped under his spell and they don't even know it. If you refuse to awaken in Jesus's name and continue to deny His resurrection power, you won't be able to pull the young people out. They don't want to do the right thing by giving God what is required from them.

After years of studying the Western church, Christian research expert George Barna has shown that "less than one out of every ten Christians age eighteen or older believes that absolute moral truth exists." Statistics in the American church for divorce rates, everyday entertainment habits, and use of medications for depression are essentially identical to those of non-Christians[22] (Stearns, p. 196). This is happening because the church is sleeping in sin, and our children need to stop believing the lies of the devil. The church is in a great depression because we don't realize that we have been lowered into the sleep in Sin Dungeon by the devil.

I don't know if you've seen the *Walking Dead* series, but God has not called us to be like the people in that series. He has called us to be sober and vigilant, because the devil is like a roaring lion, seeking whom he may devour. And yet the devil's roar is worse than his bite, so stop listening to his roar and keep your mind on Jesus Christ, the prince of peace. He will keep you in perfect peace if your mind is stayed on Him.

"By faith Enoch was taken up so that he should not see death, and he was not found, because God had taken him. Now before he was taken he was commended as having pleased God" (Hebrews 11:5). It would be nice to not have to look death in the face, if we could make this flesh subject to Jesus Christ and be consumed by thoughts of Him. If we have the faith of a mustard seed and tell that sleep-in-sin mountain to move, it shall be done. I want to have the faith of Enoch, because he didn't see death. I don't want to be lulled to sleep by satan any longer. I choose to influence my world for Jesus. I want my thoughts to line up with Jesus's thoughts.

God wants us to lay aside the weight of sin that is oppressing us. "Therefore, since we are surrounded by so great a cloud of witnesses, let us also lay aside every weight, and sin which clings so closely, and let us run with endurance the race that is set before us, looking to Jesus, the founder and perfecter of our faith, who for the joy that was set before Him endured the cross, despising the shame, and I seated at the right hand of the throne of God" (Hebrews 12:1–2).

Rahab the harlot was lulled into a deep sleep by satan, but then she was awakened by God. She had enough faith to hide God's spies when they were scoping out the land that flows with milk and honey. "By faith Rahab the prostitute did not perish with those who were disobedient, because she had given a friendly welcome to the spies" (Hebrews 11:31). "And in the same way was not also Rahab the prostitute justified by works when she received the messengers and sent them out by another way?" (James 2:25). As long as you have breath in your body, it's not too late to wake up like Rahab did.

I have received confirmation after confirmation of prophetic words that I'm supposed to be a preacher. Am I walking in my calling? No, not yet. I feel like Jonah, running from God's calling for my life. It's ironic how the Holy Spirit reveals some people's callings, but not others. I have served several churches, but nobody has ever told me that they've seen God's calling for my life and that they want to train me. However, I don't need man's approval to recognize my calling. As long as I know beyond a shadow of a doubt that God has called me into the ministry, that's all the approval I need. The Bible tells us that many are called but few are chosen. If God is for me, who can be against me?

There is no new sin under the sun. "No temptation has overtaken you except what is common to humanity. God is faithful, and He will not allow you to be tempted beyond what you are able, but with the temptation He will also provide a way of escape so that you are able to bear it" (1 Corinthians 10:13 HCSB). God is not a respecter of persons. What He did for Rahab, Enoch, and Elisha, He can do for you. You must have faith, but your faith can be as small as a mustard seed.

God said that He will keep us in perfect peace if our minds are stayed on Him. Do you realize that you are the apple of His eye? The church should keep their mind on Him and not on infirmities or sicknesses.

PART FIVE

Infirmity Spirit

~ TWENTY-TWO ~

Spirit of Infirmity

How do you know if you are in the devil's sleepwalking dungeon? When you don't know that a spirit of infirmity has you in bondage. In Luke 13:11, a woman's spirit of infirmity caused her to be bent over for eighteen years. She tried to straighten up through her own strength, but the devil kept oppressing her and wouldn't let her go. Can you imagine being tormented for eighteen years by the devil because you didn't know who was behind your infirmity?

Many of God's people are unaware that they're being tormented by the devil, but God doesn't want us to be ignorant of the devil's devices. We're supposed to test the spirit. There are so many spirits of infirmity out there, and we just accept them. If you have a sickness and you don't know where it came from, pray to God and ask the Holy Spirit to reveal it to you. Ask Him if you opened a door that has allowed that old devil to torment you. God will tell you the source of your sickness, because He doesn't want His people to be in bad health. If this spirit of infirmity was bought on by sin, then you must confess it before the Lord. "If we confess our sins, he is faithful and just to forgive us our sins, and to cleanse us from all unrighteousness" (1 John 1:9 HCBS).

"Beloved, I pray that you may prosper in all things and be in health, just as your soul prospers." (3 John 1:2 NKJV). God wants us to be in good health and not tormented by a spirit of infirmity. "And behold, there was a woman who had a spirit of infirmity eighteen years, and was bent over and could in no way raise herself up. But when Jesus saw her, he called her to Him, and said unto her, "Woman, you are loosed from your infirmity."

And He laid His hands on her, and immediately she was made straight, and glorified God." (Luke 13:11–13, NKJV).

This spirit of oppression was brought on me by willing sin; I allowed sin into the camp. Talk to God and ask Him what the culprit behind your spirit of infirmity is, and He will give you the keys to be set free. "Submit yourselves therefore to God. Resist the devil, and he will flee from you" (James 4:7). I love this scripture because it is so clear. If we submit to God and resist the devil, he will flee. The spirit of infirmity, the spirit of oppression, and any other spirit with which you are battling will have to flee in Jesus's name.

Jesus told us that we supposed to be doing greater work. He is the great teacher, healer, and savior. So why aren't we setting people free from their infirm spirits and bondage? Could it be because we are sleepwalking in sin? We must have at least the faith of a mustard seed to help people escape their infirmities. I believe that pornography, drug addiction, prostitution, alcoholism, and certain sicknesses are caused by a spirit of infirmity. You simply cannot set yourself free from those things through your own strength. That's like trying to fight a spiritual battle in the flesh, which is impossible. You need the Holy Spirit to identify the infirm spirit, and then Jesus Christ will set you free from it. But you must have the Holy Spirit living inside you.

I believe that when we are children, our spirit eyes are open to a certain extent. I remember being a child and waking up from a deep sleep at night and hearing things and seeing spirits roaming around. I remember being so scared that I screamed out loud and woke my sibling. I'm sharing this with you so that if you have experienced poltergeists or spirits, you'll know that you aren't crazy. You did see those spirits, and you weren't dreaming. One time when I was staying with my grandmother, I shared with her what I had heard. I told her that I had heard her back door open and the grate on her coal-burning potbelly stove being shaken by someone. She told me that one of neighbors, since deceased, used to come over and clean out the potbelly ashes from time to time.

If you want your spiritual eyes to open, ask God to open them. In the Old Testament, God opened the eyes of a young man so that he could see an army of angels getting ready to fight in the spirit during a battle through the prayer of Elisha. The battle is not ours. God could call down an army of angels to fight for us. "Then Elisha prayed and said, 'O Lord, please open his eyes that he may see.' So the Lord opened the eyes of the young man, and he saw, and behold, the mountain was full of horses and chariots of fire all around Elisha. And when the Syrians came down against him, Elisha prayed to the Lord and said, 'Please strike this people with blindness.' So he struck them with blindness in accordance with the prayer of Elisha" (2 King 6:17–18 ESV).

The king of Syria was warring against Israel. Syrian horses and chariots and a great host encompassed the city by night. A man of God asked Elisha what they should do, since there were more Syrians than Israelites. The man was looking through his natural eyes. So Elisha prayed to God and said, "Jehovah, I pray thee; open his eyes that he may see." So God opened the spiritual eyes of the young man, and he saw that the mountain was full of horses and chariots of fire round about Elisha, who was a prophet of God. The God I serve is not a respecter of persons. I believe that what God did for Elisha, He can do for you too. Elisha walked by faith and not by sight. I know I have warring angels encamped all around me each and every day, ready to go into battle on my behalf, if I will only pray to God to release them.

God will even open the spiritual eyes of a donkey. When God warns you not to do something, please take heed and don't do it. Balaam's greed caused him to disobey God. The Prince of Balak told his servant to tell Balaam, "I'll promote you unto very great honor." So Balaam saddled his donkey and went to the place of Moab, even after God told him not to go. God's anger was kindled toward Balaam because he had disobeyed God. "God said unto Balaam you shall go with them: you shall not curse the people; for they are blessed. The donkey saw the angel with a sword drawn in his hand ready to kill Balaam. And the donkey saw the angel of the Lord standing in the road, with a drawn sword in his hand. And the donkey turned aside out of the road and went into the field. And Balaam struck the donkey, to turn her into the road" (Numbers 22:23). The donkey ran into a wall and crushed Balaam's foot, so Balaam struck the donkey three times with his staff. Then God allowed the donkey to speak to Balaam. God had opened the donkey's spiritual eyes to see an angel with his sword drawn. Then God opened the mouth of the donkey and the donkey spoke to Balaam. "Then the Lord opened the eyes of Balaam, and he saw the angel of the Lord standing in the way, with his drawn sword in his hand. And he bowed down and fell on his face" (Numbers 22:31). God did eventually permitted Balaam to go. "And the angel of the Lord said to Balaam, 'Go with the men, but speak only the word that I tell you.' So Balaam went on with the princes of Balak" (Numbers 22:35).

When I was a kid, I remember seeing ghosts in our home. My parents used to be superstitious. They hung a horseshoe above the door to keep the ghosts at bay, but instead it kept them inside. My parents thought this kind of thinking would help them to have a problem-free life, but that was an illusion.

~ TWENTY-THREE ~

Illusion of a Problem-Free Life

How do you know if you are sleeping in sin? You are sleeping in sin when you are under the illusion that you deserve to live a problem-free life, which I call false hope. The Bible tells us that trials and tribulations will come, but that we need to be of good cheer when they do. Jesus told His disciples that they would have trouble in this world. (Read John 16:33.) As you and I know, we won't have a trouble-free life until we get to heaven.

Even in the midst of adverse circumstances, it's possible to enjoy God and glorify Him like Job did. God is interested in how you respond to those situations. For example, a temper tantrum is the wrong response, but here's the right response: "God, I know that you are in control of my life, and I trust You. You promised that You wouldn't put more on me than I can bear. So I choose to count it all joy when I encounter these various trials and tribulations." John 16:33 says, "These things I have spoken unto you, that in me ye might have peace. In the world ye shall have tribulation: but be of good cheer; I have overcome the world" (KJV).

Church, we need to stop living in fear of bad news and just remember His word to us. "Light shines in the darkness for the upright. He is gracious, compassionate, and righteous" (Psalm 112:4 HCBS). Just continue to trust in the Lord and remain steadfast. "He is not afraid of bad news; his heart is firm, trusting in the Lord. His heart is steady; he will not be afraid, until he looks in triumph on his adversaries" (Psalm 112:7–8).

Negative thoughts will cloud your mind and keep you from clearly hearing God's voice. On the other hand, if you thank Him for your trials and tribulations, then you'll hear Him loud and clear. God will keep you in perfect peace if your mind is stayed on Him. "You keep him in perfect peace whose mind is stayed on you, because he trusts in you" (Isaiah 26:3 ESV).

Focusing on your problems tends to create a barrier that keeps you from seeking God. But when you depend on Jesus, you can enjoy the abundance of life. Once you learn to keep your mind stayed on Him, then you are on the road toward learning to appreciate difficult and troubled times. Troubles will amplify your awareness of His presence, and then you will know that you have awakened from the sleep in sin. When you think that the devil is trying to lure you back into the sleep in sin, remember that God is your strength and strong tower. Then you'll stay righteous before Him, so that you can run into the strong tower and feel safe and secure. So take pleasure in leaning on Him and resting in Him.

"The thief comes only to steal and kill and destroy. I came that they may have life and have it abundantly" (John 10:10 ESV). Author Sarah Young writes in her Jesus Calling Devotion, "You know that trusting Him will bring Him to the forefront of your consciousness. So start basking in the blessing of His nearness, so His life can flow through you to others. Then you will live an abundant life. You will start seeing circumstances or troubles from His perspective and not from your perspective. Trials and tribulations will be like water on a duck's back. It will just roll off of you. Then that is when you are starting to allow the light of His presence to abundantly fill your mind and that is when you are viewing the world through Him as well as your troubles."[23]

You are allowing God to suffuse you until there is nothing left of you. Ask Him to saturate you with His presence. Ask Him to show you His Glory.

Thankfulness takes the sting out of adversity. In the book of James, we are told to count it all joy when we encounter various trials and tribulations. That's very difficult to do, especially when you're in a fiery furnace that's getting hotter and hotter. As the fiery furnace gets hotter, it will force your mind to focus on the adverse circumstances that you're facing, rather than on Jesus. I remember the story, in the third chapter of Daniel, about the three Hebrew boys who were thrown inside a hot furnace but weren't consumed. They were not focused on the hot fire, but on the fourth person who was in that furnace with them. That fourth person was Jesus. "He answered and said, 'Lo, I see four men loose, walking in the midst of the fire, and they have no hurt; and the form of the fourth is like the Son of God'" (Daniel 3:25 KJV). How will you know when you have arrived? When your mind is focused on Jesus, you aren't asleep in Sin Dungeon, and you've stop listening to the voice of the enemy. That is a great awakening.

PART SIX

The Great Awakening

~ TWENTY-FOUR ~

Foundation of Hope

On January 15, 2018, my wife and I went to a Martin Luther King Jr. Unity Awards Breakfast that was hosted by the Delta Theta Lambda Education Foundation and Delta Theta Lambda chapter. One of the guest speakers gave a dynamic testimony speech about how he had been incarcerated and come to know the Lord while in prison. God strategically placed him around a group of successful entrepreneurs and former CEOs who had gotten in trouble and ended up in prison as well, and they had taught him about business operations. This young African American guest speaker learned how to cook in prison and later became a famous chef in Las Vegas. He didn't allow his earlier mistakes to prevent him from becoming what God called him to be. He refused to let his God-given gifts lie dormant or the prison environment define him, and now he's now a celebrity chef, author, and public speaker.

His speech inspired and motivated me to get back to work on my book and return to prison ministry. That young man, who continues to go back into prisons to encourage those who are still there, woke up and stopped letting the devil destroy his life. Sometimes God will allow life situations to take you down a road that you don't want to go down. But in those down times, you can either run to God or stay bitter and throw a pity party. God does not give up on us. He gives us chance after chance to get it right.

The church needs to stop listening to the lies of the devil. He'll tell you that there's no hope for you because you'll always be a drug addict, alcoholic, adulterer, or thief. If you continue to listen to those lies, you'll be defeated. Instead, listen to what God is saying about you. God is telling you to build on a foundation of hope in Jesus Christ.

In the Bible, we read about Job's rendezvous with the devil. As usual, the devil was complaining to God about something. He had become bored with the people he could manipulate, so God asked if the devil had considered His servant Job. The devil knew that God had a hedge of protection around Job, but God agreed to lift His protection and allow the devil to do whatever he wanted to with Job, as long as the devil didn't kill Job.

So the devil had a field day tormenting Job. He took Job's sons and their families, destroyed Job's livestock, and attacked Job's body by covering him with boils from head to toe. Job's wife told him to curse God and die, but Job rebuked her because he knew that she was listening to the voice of the enemy. Not even our closest friends can comfort us when we're going through something like that. Job's friends told him that he must have sinned, since God had obviously cursed him. It's a good thing that God didn't ask the devil to consider Job's friends, because they definitely would have cursed God.

Job resided in the land of Uz. He lived a mature and upright life, fearing God and shunning evil. It's sad to think that Job was the only one in his days who feared God and obeyed His commandments. Job had a personal relationship with God and was obedient to Him, so God placed a hedge of protection around Job, his family, and his possessions. God told satan that he could do whatever he wanted to try to cause Job to stumble or curse God, as long as he didn't kill Job. Then God lifted His hedge of protection around Job and everything hit the fan.

The devil killed off Job's servants and animals. Then that old devil decided to break Job once and for all by sending a tornado to smite the four corners of the house of Job's sons and daughters. Job's sons and daughters were eating and drinking wine, having a good time in their oldest brother's house, when the devil sent the tornado through to kill them. What did Job do? He ripped his robe, shaved his head, and fell down to the ground to worship God (Job 1:20). Job understood stewardship, and he knew that he was only a steward over what God had blessed him with. I wish that we all could understand that we came into this world naked and we'll leave it naked. Anything that you receive from the Lord on this earth is temporary.

Job said, "'Naked came I out of my mother's womb, and naked shall I return thither: the Lord gave, and the Lord hath taken away; blessed be the name of the Lord.' In all this Job sinned not, nor charged God foolishly" (Job 1:21–22 KJV).

Job refused to allow the devil to lure him into his slumberous dungeon and sleep in sin. This is the kind of relationship that God wants with us—a relationship that can withstand the test of time. Job knew that the Lord gives and the Lord takes away, and that everything belongs to God anyway. God is looking for us to worship Him in the midst of our storms. God is not trying to calm the storms of life—He is trying to calm us as we go through them. The Bible tells us that trials and tribulations will come, but that we should be of good cheer.

The devil destroyed all of Job's possessions—his children, servants, and animals—but the devil didn't stop there. That wasn't sufficient torment to make Job curse God, so the devil started attacking Job's body. I wouldn't have survived what Job went through; in fact, I probably would have reminded God that He promised not to give me more than I can bear. If you're going through the fire, ask God to go with you and turn up the furnace. The devil doesn't need a reason to torment you. Job hadn't sinned, and Jesus said that the authorities hated Him without a cause, so who am I that I should escape torment?

The devil hates you because you were created in God's image, and he knows that you have been given a measure of faith. The devil is trying with all his power to prevent you from accepting Jesus as your Lord and Savior. He'll introduce you to religion, drugs, alcohol, idolatry, and so on, just to deceive you into thinking that you're okay without God. God gave satan carte blanche over Job to a certain degree, but he wasn't allowed to kill Job. So he tormented Job's body with boils from the soles of his feet to the crown of his head. Boils are very painful; they itch and burn like crazy, much like poison ivy, and they spread if you scratch them. To get some release from the painful boils, Job would sit in ashes and scrape himself with pottery fragments.

God knew that Job could bear whatever He allowed the devil to put on him, because of Job's strong relationship with God. But Job had to rebuke his wife, because she wanted him to curse God and die. Then Job's friends decided to rip their clothes and sprinkle ashes on their heads. They sat with

Job for seven days and seven nights trying to comfort him. At first they acted like true friends, because they saw that Job's grief was great. Then Job told his friends that he wished that he'd never been born. Sometime it's all right to vent, and that's what Job was doing with his friends, as we read in chapters 3 and 6.

Sometime we feel like the laughingstock of the neighborhood. Job was a perfect man, but his community was probably gossiping about him. His neighbors were probably thinking, just as his friends did, that God was mad at Job. When we see people going through something, we shouldn't judge them, because we're on the outside looking in. We can't really know what someone else is going through. Sometime we just need to pray and empathize with people. It's difficult to relate to what Job was going through, but he's a perfect example of how the church should live. Job lived a life in good standing with the Lord, he didn't complain to his neighbors, and he loved people from all walks of life.

Job's sickness came from the devil. When sickness attacks your body, pray to the Lord and He will reveal to you where your sickness comes from and what you need to do to rebuke it. Rely totally on God for answers to any illnesses or problems that you are facing, but don't blame God for them. Job didn't do that, because he had a strong relationship with God. God does allow the devil to attack our bodies sometimes, just like He allowed the devil to attack Job's body. Sometimes God will let the devil attack your family and possessions, just to make certain that you're keeping the Lord first in your life. "But seek ye first the kingdom of God, and His righteousness; and all these things shall be added unto you" (Matthew 6:33). The devil has to get God's permission before he can do anything to God's children, because we're under God's umbrella of protection.

The devil hates God and His children, especially those who are obedient and faithful to the Lord. The devil hates your faithful relationship and fellowship with God. The devil doesn't want you to wake up; that's why he keeps sending fiery darts your way. The devil accuses us before God and says, "If You let me touch their bones or their body, they will curse you to your face." If you have a healthy fear of God and live in good standing with Him, the Lord will keep His umbrella of protection around you unless you blatantly sin. "But the mercy of the Lord is from everlasting to everlasting On those who fear Him, And His righteousness to children's children" (Psalm 103:17 NKJV).

Job's friends didn't sympathize with him because they couldn't relate to what he was going through, even though Job begged them to show him mercy (Job 19:21). When we're going through something, it can feel like God has forsaken us. Even Jesus felt that way, because He was fully human. When He was on the cross, Jesus cried, "My God! My God! Why have You forsaken me?" Jesus felt like the burden was too much for Him to bear, so he asked God to let that cup pass from Him.

When you are at the lowest point in your life, people will condemn you, like Job's friends condemned him. "Also against his three friends was his wrath kindled, because they had found no answer, and yet had condemned Job" (Job 32:3). But Jesus will never condemn us. "For God sent not his Son into the world to condemn the world; but that the world through him might be saved" (John 3:17 KJV).

Even while you're in the devil's slumberous dungeon of sin, God is still speaking to you. "For God speaketh once, yea twice, yet man perceiveth it not. In a dream, in a vision of the night, when deep sleep falleth upon men, in slumberings upon the bed; Then he openeth the ears of men, and sealeth their instruction, That he may withdraw man from his purpose, and hide pride from man. He keepeth back his soul from the pit, and his life from perishing by the sword" (Job 33:14–18 KJV). This is the kind of God that I want to serve—one who will speak to me even when the enemy has lulled me into a deep-sleeping dungeon. God will deliver you from going down to the pit. "Then he is gracious unto him, and saith, Deliver him from going down to the pit: I have found a ransom" (Job 33:24 KJV). If you go into the pit, God will bring you back out. "To bring back his soul from the pit, to be enlightened with the light of the living" (Job 33:30 KJV).

It's easy to be like Job's friends and think that your sin is the reason something bad is happening to you. "My servant Job will pray for you, and I will accept his prayer on your behalf. I will treat you as you deserve, for you have not spoken accurately about me, as my servant Job has." (Job 42:, NLT). "After the Lord had spoken these words to Job, the Lord said to Eliphaz the Temanite, 'My anger burns against you and against your two friends, for you have not spoken of me what is right, as my servant Job has'" (Job 42:7, ESV). If you make a statement about what God said, make sure that it's accurate, because the Lord will rebuke you like He did Job's friends. Sometimes we think we're hearing what the Lord is saying, when actually we don't hear Him correctly.

The church is terrible about comforting people who are going through something difficult. It's easy to judge people and assume that they must have sinned or done something to make God mad at them. Sometimes we just need to be quiet and pray without ceasing. In order to encourage people who are going through something, the church needs to do more declaring: Walk in the fruit of the spirit, flee from negativity and attract positivity, and the power of darkness will have no more influence over you. Refuse to succumb to satan's sleepwalking spell ever again. Speak up for righteousness in love. Declare the hope of glory, especially when you feel hopeless. You can survive every shipwreck that the adversary sends your way, in Jesus's name.

There's a treasure chest inside you that symbolizes the building materials of glory. You will be a vessel of honor, a symbol that represents strength, courage, and boldness. Always remember that God honors those who fear Him.[24]

> Know that God will pick you up out of any situation and place a mark of honor, esteem, and favor for others to respect. You are not a rug to be walked over but a person with real feelings and a real heart. God will shield you from any evil intentions as you continue to stand on His rock-solid promises. God will perfect those things concerning you. God will give you His perfect will for your life in His Word. God will help you walk in prophetic fulfillment for your life. The enemy wants to pervert your destiny, but God overrides and veto his plan and God will perfect your destiny.[25]

Job stayed in constant communication with God, to help him live above his circumstances even while he was in the midst of them. Job was declaring that "I can do all things through Christ who strengthens me" (Philippians 4:13).

After the condemnation from Job's friends, God got tired of Job's bellyaching and chewed Him out. "Then answered the Lord unto Job out of the whirlwind, and said, Gird up thy loins now like a man: I will demand of thee, and declare thou unto me" (Job 40:6–7 KJV). God told Job to man up and stop his bellyaching. Whatever you're going through, ask God to give you the strength and endurance to persevere.

God gave Job double for his trouble at the end of his storm. "So the Lord blessed the latter end of Job more than his beginning: for he had fourteen thousand sheep, and six thousand camels, and a thousand yoke of oxen, and a thousand she asses" (Job 42:12 KJV). God let Job see four generations. "After this lived Job an hundred and forty years, and saw his sons, and his sons' sons, even four generations. So Job died, being old and full of days" (Job 42:16–17 KJV). If the Lord tarries, I pray that He will allow me to see four generations, but in good health. "His flesh shall be fresher than a child's: he shall return to the days of his youth: He shall pray unto God, and he will be favourable unto him: and he shall see his face with joy: for he will render unto man his righteousness" (Job 33:25–26 KJV).

As the Lord tarries, the Antichrist could appear, so the church needs to be equipped. When the Antichrist comes, he will deceive many people, even some of the elect.

~ TWENTY-FIVE ~

Recognizing the Antichrist

How can you recognize the Antichrist if you are walking in the sleep in sin? What better time for the Antichrist to make an appearance than when the church has fallen asleep? I don't know about you, but I don't want to be deceived by the Antichrist. God wants the church to awaken so that we can recognize the Antichrist when he appears. "Children, it is the last hour, and as you have heard that antichrist is coming, so now many antichrists have come. Therefore we know that it is the last hour" (1 John 2:18 ESV). Church, I am here to warn you that this is the last hour and we need to experience a great awakening.

The scriptures tell us how to recognize the Antichrist when he shows up. "Who is the liar but he who denies that Jesus is the Christ? This is the antichrist, he who denies the Father and the Son" (1 John 2:22 ESV). The Antichrist will never confess that Jesus is the Son of God and that Jesus and the Father are one. If you're still unsure, then test the spirits:

> Beloved, do not believe every spirit, but test the spirits to see whether they are from God, for many false prophets have gone out into the world. By this you know the Spirit of God: every spirit that confesses that Jesus Christ has come in the flesh is from God, and every spirit that does not confess Jesus is not from God. This is the spirit of the antichrist, which you heard was coming and now is in the world already. Little children, you are from God and have overcome them, for he who is in you is greater

than he who is in the world. They are from the world; therefore they speak from the world, and the world listens to them. We are from God. Whoever knows God listens to us; whoever is not from God does not listen to us. By this we know the Spirit of truth and the spirit of error. (1 John 4:1–6 ESV)

When the Antichrist does come, he will sit on the throne of David. (Read the book of Revelation and 2 Thessalonians 2.)

Why are you letting your religious thinking trick you into believing that Jesus is not the Son of God? The devil knows the truth, but he doesn't want you to know the truth, so he convinced you that religion can get you into heaven. The devil knows that Jesus is the Son of God. That's why the devil came to Jesus after forty days of fasting and tried to tempt Jesus into worshipping him. The devil appeared before Jesus three times trying to cause Jesus to sin. The devil knew that he was wasting his time, but he tried anyway.

The church should imitate Christ. When the devil comes toward us with his fiery little darts of temptation, we should not yield. The gospels of Matthew, Mark, Luke, and John talk about how satan tried to tempt Jesus but failed at every attempt. Jesus was confident in His identity, and we should be too. Our identity is in Jesus. Jesus didn't entertain the lies of the enemy, and neither should we.

This generation should tell the devil to shut up and go back to hell where he belongs. Tell the devil that you refuse to be his puppet on a string any longer. Tell him that you refuse to be his slave any longer. If you declare these things, then watch that old devil and his demons hightail it out of here. If you really want the devil to leave you alone, do what Jesus did when He said, "Be gone, satan! For it is written, you shall worship the Lord your God and Him only shall you serve" (Matthew 4:10). When you command the devil to flee in Jesus's name without doubting, he will have to flee.

In Matthew 4, notice all the ammo that the devil threw at Jesus after Jesus's forty-day fast. The first temptation was the lust of the flesh. The devil wanted Jesus to turn a stone into bread, because he knew that Jesus had fasted for forty days and forty nights. The second temptation the devil threw at Jesus was the pride of life. The devil took Jesus to the holy city and set Him on the pinnacle of the temple. Then the devil said to Jesus, "If you are the Son of God throw yourself down; for it is written, 'He will give His angels charge concerning you'" (Matthew 4:6). That old devil tried to get Jesus to commit suicide and to tempt the Lord, thou God. Of course, Jesus didn't fall for it; He would never let pride of life hinder Him from His mission. The devil's ego is so big that he wanted Jesus to obey him and not God.

The devil thought that he could trip Jesus up by using the Word, but Jesus is the living Word of God. "In the beginning was the Word, and the Word was with God, and the Word was God. He was in the beginning with God. All things were made through him, and without him was not anything made that was made. In him was life, and the life was the light of men. The light shines in the darkness, and the darkness has not overcome it" (John 1:1–5 ESV). If we are in Christ Jesus, we should have the Word living inside of us. But we're letting that old devil continue to trick us, because we are walking in the sleep in Sin Dungeon.

Notice the scripture verse that says, "All things were made through him." We were made through Jesus Christ. If Jesus didn't yield to the devil's temptations, then why should we? We should stop listening to the enemy's lies, because suicide is just the trick of the enemy. The devil knows that we were created in the image of God, and he doesn't like it.

The last temptation the devil tried on Jesus was the lust of the eyes. The devil took Jesus to a high mountain and showed Him all the kingdoms of the world and their glory. Then the devil said, "'All these things I will give to you, if you will fall down and worship me. Jesus looked at the devil like he was stupid, and Jesus told the devil, "Be gone, satan!'" (Matthew 4:9–10). Jesus had heard enough from satan. Jesus knew that God was the creator of everything, the heavens and earth, so it all belongs to Him. Jesus knew that the Father and He are one, so everything the Father created belongs to Jesus.

Church, if everything belongs to Jesus, then it also belongs to you. Stop falling for the lust of the flesh, lust of the eyes, and the pride-of-life fiery darts that the devil keeps throwing at you. We need to start telling the devil, "Be gone, satan!" and watch that sucker flee like lightning. When the devil whispers in your ear and tells you to commit suicide, say to him, "Be gone, satan!" When he tells you to continue hating, using illegal drugs, committing adultery, drinking, lying, using pornography, and walking in unforgiveness, just tell him, "Be gone, satan!" in Jesus's name and watch him flee. "For in that he himself hath suffered being tempted, he is able to succour them that are tempted" (Hebrews 2:18 KJV). If the enemy tried to tempt Jesus, he will try to tempt you too.

Imagine yourself free from bondage. Start seeing yourself the way God sees you—free from hurt, shame, and disappointments. Imagine yourself free from illegal drugs, pornography, sexual immorality, lying, and so on. By living in freedom, you are living a victorious life. Amen!

We don't know the day or hour when Jesus is coming. So we need to stay awake, stop sleeping in sin, and stop letting the devil trip us up. Without Christ, we are just empty vessels. "Therefore, stay awake, for you do not know on what day your Lord is coming" (Matthew 24:42 ESV).

Mark 13:33–35 tells us to be on guard by staying awake. If the master of the house goes on a journey and leaves a servant in charge, then the servant commands the doorkeeper to stay alert, because they don't know when the master will return. But when the cat's away, the mice will play. The servant decides to throw a wild party, so the doorkeeper has to keep watch for the master, because the servant doesn't want the master to return unexpectedly and catch the servant disrespecting his master's home.

Ephesians 5:14 tells us, "Awake, O Sleeper, and arise from the dead, and Christ will shine on you." I need Christ to shine in every area of my life and bring my hidden sins into the light so that I can be set free from bondage.

First Thessalonians 5:5–6 says, "We are children of light. We are no longer children of darkness. So let us no longer sleep, as others do, but let us keep awake and be sober." We need to keep wearing the breastplate of faith and love, and for a helmet the hope of salvation. The church needs to stop sleeping in sin by pleasing the flesh, so that we'll recognize the Antichrist when he appears on the scene. The time is drawing near when Christ will return for His bride. If the church is still sleeping in sin, why should Jesus come back to a bride who has blemishes and lives in sin? God's Word tells us to remember where we have fallen and repent. God continues to warn His people to repent and wake up. (Read 2 Thessalonians 2:7–12.)

Revelation 16:15 says, "Behold I am coming like a thief! Blessed is the one who stays awake, keeping his garments on that he may not go about naked and be seen exposed!" Jesus is coming back like a thief. We will not know the day or hour. Jesus said that only the Father knows when He will be returning for the church. It's imperative that we keep His garments on and take off our fleshly garments. Wouldn't it be nice to know when a thief plans to break into your home so that you could prepare for him?

If there is not a great awakening soon in the church, our identity will be whatever the devil wants—drug addict, alcoholic, fornicator, pervert, and so on. But if the church finally awakens from the sleep in sin, our identity in Christ will be faithful servant, royal priest, ambassador for Christ, beloved, and overcomer. We'll be walking in the Spirit instead of fulfilling the lust of the flesh. Because of the never-ending, reckless love of our God, He will leave the ninety-nine just to find one and bring him back home. The God we serve throws all of our sins into the sea of forgetfulness. Isn't that awesome?

The church's main responsibility is to remain alert for the return of Jesus and let Him lead and guide us. I know that sounds elementary, but it's not. Our desire to live in His presence goes against the grain of this world, our flesh, and the devil, so don't grow weary in your constant battle against those opponents.

The church needs to be wise about the entrapments of the enemy. If we perpetually walk in the Spirit, we don't have to worry about fulfilling the lust of the flesh like Shechem did: "And when Shechem the son of Hamor the Hivite, prince of the country, saw her, he took her and lay with her, and violated her" (Genesis 34:2). Shechem was consumed by the lust of the flesh, which caused him to rape Dinah, the daughter of Leah and Jacob. After Shechem had violated Dinah, he asked his father to request her as his wife. When Jacob heard about what Shechem had done to his daughter, he was outraged, but he kept his peace.

Jacob sons, however, didn't keep their peace. Simeon and Levi, Dinah's brothers, were out in the fields tending to their livestock when the incident occurred. When they heard the disgraceful thing that the Shechem had done to their sister, they got very angry. It's obvious to me that the Shechem was spoiled and used to getting what he wanted when he wanted it. To make matters worse, Shechem's father tried to dictate to Jacob that his son would marry Dinah after the fact. Shechem said to Jacob, Simeon, and Levi, "Let me find favor in your eyes, and whatever you say to me I will give" (Genesis 34:11). But Dinah's brothers told Shechem that they couldn't give their sister to an uncircumcised man, because that would be a reproach to Israel.

However, they said that if Shechem and every other male would get circumcised, then they would give Dinah to Shechem as his wife. That was a bald-faced lie, but the stupid man didn't even realize it. Jacob was a deceitful shyster, and the apple doesn't fall too far from the tree. Shechem and his father fell for the lie and got circumcised, but while they were recuperating, Simeon and Levi went in with a sword and killed Hamor, Shechem, and all the other men in Hivite. This is a sad, sad story.

So why didn't God warn Jacob about the rape so that he could have prevented it? The spirit of deception flowed from Jacob down to his children as a generational curse. Simeon and Levi deceived Shechem the Hivite, and later they deceived Jacob when they told him that Joseph had been killed by a wild beast. They couldn't tell their father the truth about his favorite son. That's how sin operates—you have to keep covering it up with lies upon lies. Why do you suppose Jacob didn't question his sons about Joseph's coat of many colors? His sons had sprinkled blood on the coat, but it hadn't been ripped to shreds.

Don't ever move out from under God's umbrella of protection. God knows how to protect His children. Genesis 49:5 says, "Simeon and Levi are brothers; weapons of violence are their swords." Genesis 49:7 says, "Cursed be their anger, for it is fierce, and their wrath, for it is cruel! I will divide them in Jacob and scatter them in Israel." Simeon and Levi were so angry at what Shechem had done to their sister, but God cursed their anger.

Do not take matters in your own hand like Simeon and Levi did. Jesus is our vindicator. So, allow the resurrection power that raised Jesus from the dead vindicate for you.

~ TWENTY-SIX ~

Resurrection Power

I have some good news to share with you. We don't have to sleep in the enemy's Sin Dungeon any longer. God has given us everything we need to be snatched from the snares of the enemy. The same resurrection power that raised Jesus from the dead resides in us. If we really want to silence the voice of the enemy, then we need to tell that old devil to get back under our feet where he belongs.

Have you ever tried to talk with someone who has their hands around your throat? It's very difficult. Paul wrote to the Philippians, "That I may know Him and the power of His resurrection, and may share His sufferings, becoming like Him in His death, that by any means possible I may attain the resurrection from the dead" (Philippians 3:10–11). If Jesus lives inside us, we can attain the same resurrection power that raised Him from the dead. Church, we have no excuse to continue sleeping in sin. We are no longer bound by chains and darkness, because of what Jesus did two thousand years ago. We can choose to continue to sleep in sin, but if we're ready to experience the great awakening, now is the time.

The devil doesn't want us to know that we have resurrection power. That's why he wants us to continue sleeping in Sin Dungeon. The devil doesn't want us to experience a great awakening, but God has given us everything we need to finish the race. We just need to decide to wake up, but if we continue to walk in the sleep in sin, we should prepare to face the consequences. "For many, of whom I have often told you and now tell you even with tears, walk as enemies of the cross of Christ. Their end is destruction, their god is their belly, and they glory in their shame, with minds set on earthly things" (Philippians 3:18–19 ESV). Church, it's high time that we get our minds off earthly things and focus on heavenly things. God doesn't want any of His people to perish. Paul goes on to say, "But our citizenship is in heaven, and from it we await a Savior, the Lord Jesus Christ, who will transform our lowly body to be like his glorious body, by the power that enables him even to subject all things to himself" (Philippians 3:20–21 ESV).

We need to experience a great awakening, "so as to walk in a manner worthy of the Lord, fully pleasing to him: bearing fruit in every good work and increasing in the knowledge of God; being strengthened with all power, according to his glorious might, for all endurance and patience with joy" (Colossians 1:10–11 ESV). Church, we're supposed to be walking by faith and not by sight. Pray this prayer with me if you are ready to experience a great awakening:

> Father, I thank you for the resurrection power that you have given me to raise those things that were dead or walking in the sleep in sin in my life. I thank You for equipping and strengthening me with all power to walk out of this sleep in Sin Dungeon and no longer be bound in chains and darkness. I choose from this day forward to be sober and vigilant through Your resurrection power, which lives inside me, and live a victorious life. I am no longer bound by sleep in sin and darkness, in Jesus's name. I choose on this day to experience the great awakening once and for all, with the Holy Spirit residing in me, in Jesus's name. I choose to silence the voice of the enemy from this day forward, by keeping the enemy under my feet where he belongs. I choose to no longer be bound by dead things such as alcohol addiction, drug addiction, pornography, fornication, perversion, sexual immorality, greed, lust of the flesh, lust of the eyes, and pride of life. All of those dead things must flee in Jesus's name. I choose this day to walk in a manner worthy of the Lord and fully pleasing to Him, bearing the fruit of the Spirit—love, joy, peace, patience, kindness, goodness, faithfulness,

gentleness, and self-control. From this day forward, I choose to give the Holy Spirit full control of my life, in Jesus's name. Amen!

Jesus said to her (being Martha), "I am the resurrection and the life, whoever believes in Me, though he die, yet shall he live" (John 11:25, ESV). Although we are bound by the enemy's sleep in sin, Jesus wants us to experience the great awakening through His resurrection power.

If you choose to remain in asleep in sin, the spirit of the Sadducees and Pharisees will overtake you. "For the Sadducees say that there is no resurrection, nor angel, nor spirit, but the Pharisees acknowledge them all" (Acts 23:8 ESV). That spirit of religion overtook the Sadducees to the point that they didn't believe in the resurrection power, though the Pharisees did. It's really sad to think that people will allow the spirit of religion to keep them bound. Those are the people who stayed in the church, but they did not have a relationship with God the Father. How could someone live in the church without realizing that the enemy has them spellbound in the sleep in sin?

The spirit of religion will choke the life out of you and sell you a one-way ticket to hell. The Pharisees and Sadducees hardened their hearts so much that Jesus couldn't save them when He was walking on the earth. When Jesus comes, I pray that you will not harden your heart. Let Jesus shine His Light in those areas of your life from which you cannot break free. If you expose the devil, then you'll know how to oppose him. So I beseech you to turn those dead things, your hidden sins, over to Jesus Christ. Those are the things that keep you from growing in the knowledge of Jesus Christ.

Ask Jesus to let His will be done in your life. If you leave your hidden sins at the foot of the cross, He will throw them into the sea of forgetfulness. Just say, "Jesus, I want you to set me free from ..." You might want to be set free from drugs, alcohol, cigarettes, pornography, fornication, sexual immorality, greed, lasciviousness, and so on. Whatever it is, just turn it over to Jesus. The devil will fight to keep you in bondage, but you have the same resurrection power that raised Jesus from the dead. Keep telling yourself that you can do all things through Christ, who strengthens you. If you want to accomplish something, you have to believe that you can do it. If you want to become a professional athlete, you have to practice, practice, practice—and believe in yourself. Likewise, if you want to be set free from the sleep in sin, you have to believe in the resurrection power that lives inside you.

I pray that the great awakening comes soon for the sake of our children and their children. "Then Jesus said to them, 'You will all fall away because of me this night. For it is written, "I will strike the shepherd, and the sheep of the flock will be scattered." But after I am raised up, I will go before you to Galilee'" (Matthew 26:31 ESV). Pastor, you know that if you make one mistake, the enemy will cause your sheep to scatter. One of the mega-church pastors experienced this just recently. If one of your sheep tells you that they will never fall away, they are in denial. Peter said that he would never forsake Jesus, but Jesus told him that before the rooster crowed, Peter would deny him three times.

That's why we need to stand fortified and of one accord. The church needs to say to the enemy, "If you strike one, you strike us all." We refuse to allow any of our wounded soldiers to fall and be trampled upon. God didn't call us to hide our heads in the sand and pretend that we don't see what's going on in the world. He called us to be bold: "The wicked flee when no one pursues, but the righteous are bold as a lion" (Proverbs 28:1 ESV). He called us to have confidence: "Is not your fear of God your confidence, and the integrity of your ways your hope?" (Job 4:6 ESV). And He called us to be courageous: "Be strong and courageous. Do not fear or be in dread of them, for it is the Lord your God who goes with you. He will not leave you or forsake you" (Deuteronomy 31:6 ESV). So let us walk by faith and not by sight. When you have God-fearing boldness on your life, that is when you can say, "I can do all things through Christ who strengthen me." "A wicked man puts on a bold face, but the upright gives thought to his ways" (Proverbs 21:29 ESV).

Paul said in Philippians 1:6, "And I am confident (sure) of this, that He who began a good work in you will bring it to completion at the day of Jesus Christ."

We know we have a great awakening by how we treat one another. If we treat people the way God treats and sees people, we are not asleep in sin. If we treat people like their lives are not valuable, we are asleep in sin. We should treat people the way we want to be treated. When you are at a crossroads and have to decide how you should treat people who are different from you, ask God to show you how to make wise choices. Man looks at the color of your skin. God looks at the heart.

Billy Graham's daughter Anne Graham Lotz was interviewed on the *Early Show* after the attacks on the Twin Towers and the Pentagon on September 11, 2001. "How could God let something like this happen?" the interviewer asked. Graham Lotz gave an extremely profound and insightful response: "I believe God is deeply saddened by this just as we are, but for years we've been telling God to get out of our schools, to get out of our government, and to get out of our lives. And being the gentleman He is, I believe He has calmly backed out. How can we expect God to give us His blessing and His protection if we demand Him to leave us alone?" In light of recent events, terrorists attack, school shootings, et cetera, I think it started when Madalyn Murray O'Hair (she was murdered, her body found recently) complained she didn't want prayer in our schools, and we said okay. Then someone said you better not read the Bible in school ... The Bible says thou shalt not kill, thou shalt not steal, and love your neighbor as yourself. And we said okay. Then Dr. Benjamin Spock said we shouldn't spank our children when they misbehave because their little personalities would be warped and we might damage their self-esteem. (Dr. Spock's son committed suicide.) We said an expert should know what he's talking about. And we said okay. Now we're asking ourselves why our children have no conscience, why they don't know right from wrong, and why it doesn't bother them to kill strangers, their classmates, and themselves. Probably if we think about it long and hard enough, we can figure it out. I think it has a great deal to do with 'We reap what we sow.' Funny how simple it is for people to trash God and then wonder why the world's going to hell. Funny how we believe what the newspaper says, but question what the Bible says. Funny how you can send 'jokes' through e-mail and they spread like wildfire but when you start sending messages regarding the Lord, people think twice about sharing. Funny how lewd, crude, vulgar, and obscene articles pass freely through cyberspace, but public discussion of God is suppressed in the school and workplace."[26]

Dr. Spock's advice on not disciplining your child goes against the grain of the Word of God. God said, "Spare the rod, spoil the child." When you have a spoiled child, you cannot control them. They are angry and bitter all the time, throw temper tantrums, and will not listen to authority figures, teachers, parents, police officers, and so on. It is not too late to put prayer and paddling back into the schools. I got spankings growing up when I misbehaved at home and at school. It didn't warp my mind. It taught me to respect authority figures. It taught me to love. Yes, the spanking hurt for a little while, but you can rest assured I didn't make the same mistake twice. A child doesn't know any better. If you don't discipline them then, how will they know what is wrong and what is right? If you saw your child running over to a fire, would you not stop them? We're supposed to be training our children in the way they should go. Then when they are older, they will not depart from our ways. We're supposed to be teaching our children and keeping them from injuring themselves.

Why do we trust one human being's advice when they are a human being like us? Why do we refuse to trust the one who created the world and the universe even though He has the whole world in the palm of His hand? When we force God out of our lives, we don't have any protection from the enemy. We are like a sitting duck. I remember a time when I wanted to live selfishly. I told God to leave me alone. The devil knew God had a protection around me. He wanted me to denounce the protection, because that was the only way he could get to me. God is a respecter of people, and a gentleman. God respected my wish. So when I declared that, a great spirit of depression came over me. I didn't know if I was coming or going. Those demons were tormenting me and trying to destroy me. But in the midst of this great depression I was still going to church. I didn't tell anyone what I was going through. I was fighting this battle on my own. I was still praying to God, but I wanted to live my life as though I were suicidal or playing Russian roulette. But thanks be to God, who led me into triumph. I kept a channel open with Him, and that was how I was able to fight this battle. The devil comes to kill, steal, and destroy, but Jesus came to give us life and life more abundantly.

I am still sleeping in sin. God told me by prophetic words that I am going to do great things for His kingdom, but they are lying dormant. He told me I am going to influence the lives of thousands of boys and men. Then my wife and I got another prophetic word that we are getting ready to explode like a volcano that has lain dormant for years. God is shaking and stirring in us a mixture that has been dormant for years, and now it is getting ready to explode.

God is restoring to you what the locusts ate and destroyed in Joel 2:25. The locusts could be drugs, alcohol, prison, or hatred; you can fill in the locust word that has kept you in bondage. Many have counted you out of the game, but God never created you to be defined by defeats or disappointments or discouragements. You are a prime example of an overcomer. Always take negative criticism as a compliment. God said He will restore what you've lost and reconstruct that which has been torn down. God will build you up like a fortified wall that is impenetrable. God is your strong tower and dwelling place. The name of the Lord is a strong tower. The righteous run in and they are safe.[27] God said that when you are weak and need spiritual nourishment, He will bring the milk and meat of the nations to you. (Read 1 Peter 2:3–6, Proverbs 18:10, and Psalm 61:3.)

Church, the sleeping giant, what does it take for us to experience an awakening? "He will not allow your foot to slip; your Protector will not slumber. Indeed, the Protector of Israel does not slumber or sleep" (Psalm 121:3–4 HCSB). If we are in Christ Jesus, then why are we allowing the enemy to keep us asleep in sin? God is our protector, but we have to trust Him and stay under His umbrella of protection. If you only stop believing the lies of the enemy that keep you asleep in sin, you will not sin.

The reason why the devil wants you stay asleep in sin is that he doesn't want you to find that secret place with God. This is the place where the devil cannot enter. This is the place where God will wrap His arms around you and reveal to you His heart. In this secret place God can really show you His glory. This secret place is where you are alone in His presence and all you can do is fall on your knees and cry out, "Cleanse me with Your fire and purify my heart." This secret place is where God can draw you close—closer than before and closer than you've ever been. This secret place should be your heart's only desire. The devil is trying his hardest to keep you out of that secret place by sifting you from it. This secret place is where God can make you be like Him in the Spirit. "Simon, Simon, behold, satan demanded to have you, that he might sift you like wheat, but I have prayed for you that your faith may not fail. And when you have turned again, strengthen your brothers" (Luke 22:31–32 ESV). If you want to know the heart of God, I challenge you to experience the great awakening and go to that secret place where God will reveal to you His heart. "In distress you called, and I delivered you; I answered you in the secret place of thunder" (Psalm 81:6 ESV).

~ TWENTY-SEVEN ~

Awakening the Sleeping Giant

The church has to read the writing on the wall and listen to what the Holy Spirit is saying to her. God is telling us that it is high time to awaken from the sleep in sin. "Besides this you know the time, that the hour has come for you to wake from sleep. For salvation is nearer to us now than when we first believed. The night is far gone; the day is at hand. So then let us cast off the works of darkness and put on the armor of light. Let us walk properly as in the daytime, not in orgies and drunkenness, not in sexual immorality and sensuality, not in quarreling and jealousy. But put on the Lord Jesus Christ, and make no provision for the flesh, to gratify its desires" (Romans 13:11–14 ESV). Many lives are hanging in the balance, ready to be snatched from the snares of the enemy. Even your soul is hanging in the balance. God wants the church to start walking properly and respectfully again and do away with the illicit orgies, drunkenness, sexual immorality and sensuality, quarreling and jealousy, gossiping, backbiting, fornication, and drugs. In other words, God wants us to put back on the Lord Jesus Christ, and stop making provision for the flesh and gratifying its desires. When God warns the church to awaken, we had better heed the warning. *Matthew Henry's Concise Commentary* addresses the consequences of our continuing to sleep in sin:

> Four things are here taught, as a Christian's directory for his day's work. When to awake; Now; and to awake out of the sleep of carnal security, sloth, and negligence; out of the sleep of spiritual death, and out of the sleep of spiritual

deadness. Considering the time; a busy time; a perilous time. Also, the salvation nigh at hand. Let us mind our way, and mend our pace, we are nearer our journey's end. Also, to make ourselves ready. The night is far spent, the day is at hand; therefore, it is time to dress ourselves. Observe what we must put off; clothes worn in the night. Cast off the sinful works of darkness. Observe what we must put on; how we should dress our souls. Put on the armor of light. A Christian must reckon himself undressed, if unarmed. The graces of the Spirit are this armor, to secure the soul from satan's temptations, and the assaults of this present evil world. Put on Christ; that includes all. Put on righteousness of Christ, for justification. Put on the Spirit and grace of Christ, for sanctification. The Lord Jesus Christ must be put on as Lord to rule you as Jesus to save you; and in both, as Christ anointed and appointed by the Father to this ruling, saving work. And how to walk. When we are up and ready, we are not to sit still, but to appear abroad; let us walk. Christianity teaches us how to walk so as to please God, whoever sees us. Walk honestly as in the day; avoiding the works of darkness. Where there are riot and drunkenness, there usually are chambering and wantonness, and strife and envy. Solomon puts these all together, Proverbs 23:29–35. See what provision to make. Our great care must be to provide for our souls: but must we take no care about our bodies? Yes; but two things are forbidden. Perplexing ourselves with anxious, encumbering care; and indulging ourselves in irregular desires. Natural wants are to be answered, but evil appetites must be checked and denied. To ask meat for our necessities, is our duty, we are taught to pray for daily bread; but to ask meat for our lusts, is provoking God, Psalm 78:18.[28]

God doesn't want any of His children to perish, but we have to awaken from the sleep in sin. It is time to start influencing our city, our state, our country, and this world. God wants us to be virtuous and respectable people. "Take no part in the unfruitful works of darkness, but instead expose them" (Ephesians 5:11 ESV). If you expose the devil, then you will know how to oppose him. God even tells us, "Do not speak of those shameful things that they did in secret" (Ephesians 5:12). When you are asleep in sin, those shameful things are a part of you and you cannot distinguish between what is wrong and what is right. But God wants to expose those things that are choking the life out of you.

In Ephesians 5:13 God says that those things you do in secret will be exposed by the light and become visible. God doesn't want you to be traduced by those things. He wants you to be blameless. Why does God want to expose those shameful things that you do in secret? Because He loves you. He wants you to remain under His umbrella of protection. "For anything that becomes visible is light. Therefore it says, 'Awake, O sleeper, and arise from the dead, and Christ will shine on you'" (Ephesians 5:14 ESV). God wants you to rise from those dead things that are choking the life out of you.

For the church to have a great awakening, we must repent and turn from our wicked ways. Jesus wants to shine on you, church. As you know, we are in evil times when people do not understand the value of a human life. We are in the time when anything goes. How many times have you heard, "If it feels good, do it"? God wants you to "Look carefully then how you walk, not as unwise but as wise, making the best use of the time, because the days are evil" (Ephesians 5:15 ESV). God wants you to walk as children of light (for the fruit of light is found in all that is good and right and true) and not in the sleep in sin (darkness) and try to discern what is pleasing to the Lord. You cannot discern what is pleasing to the Lord if you are walking in darkness. If you continue to walk in the sleep in sin, you are being foolish like the five foolish virgins, but if you walk in wisdom, you are being like the five wise virgins. By walking like the five wise virgins, you understand the will of the Lord for you. His will for you is to live a virtuous life, so that He can say, "Well done, my faithful servant." This is a life that is pleasing in His sight. God is omnipresent (all powerful), omniscient (all knowing), and omnipotent (all powerful). So He sees those things you do in secret. He knows those things that you are thinking in your mind.

Paul said in Romans 7:15, "For I do not understand my own actions. For I do not do what I want, but I do the very thing I hate. Now if I do what I do not want, I agree with the law, that it is good. So now it is no longer I who do it, but sin that dwells within me. For I know that nothing good dwells in me, that is, in my flesh. For I have the desire to do what is right, but not the ability to carry it out. For I do not do the good I want, but the evil I do not want is what I keep on doing. Now if I do what I do not want, it is no longer I who do it, but sin that dwells within me" (Romans 7:15–20 ESV). The devil has brought on the sleep in sin that is controlling you, but you do not realize it. That is how cunning he is. The devil will cause you to do the things you hate, which are those fleshly desires. That is the reason why God wants the church to awaken. so we will stop fulfilling the lust of the flesh, the lust of the eyes, and the pride of life. Those things are hostile to God, who continues to warn us about pleasing the flesh and sleeping in sin.

God wants the church to awaken so we can inherit His kingdom. If the church refuses to awaken and continues down the path of pleasing the flesh, then we will not inherit His kingdom. You know what the works of the flesh are. "Now the works of the flesh are evident: sexual immorality, impurity, sensuality, idolatry, sorcery, enmity, strife, jealousy, fits of anger, rivalries, dissensions, divisions, envy, drunkenness, orgies, and things like these. I warn you, as I warned you before, that those who do such things will not inherit the kingdom of God" (Galatians 5:19–21 ESV). God is continually warning us about pleasing the flesh and sleeping in sin. How many times must God warn us? He gave Sodom and Gomorrah ample time to repent, but they didn't heed His warning. Even in the days of Noah, He gave them ample time to repent. "Knowing God's thoughts toward you daily will ignite the sleeping giant on the inside of you and take giant leaps of faith."[29]

So, I beseech you to awaken and remain in Christ Jesus. Jesus crucified the flesh with its passion and desires. If we see our brother in Christ in blatant sin, we should love him enough to restore him with a spirit of gentleness. I believe this is one of the gifts from the Holy Spirit. Love covers a multitude of sin. "If we confess our sins, He is faithful and just to forgive us our sins and to cleanse us from all unrighteousness" (John 1:9 ESV). But we've got to be awakened so He can stir up the gifts He deposited inside of you. God always gives us a way to escape, if we just take advantage of it. Isn't that good news?

~ TWENTY-EIGHT ~

Gifts from the Holy Spirit

"For John truly baptized with water; but ye shall be baptized with the Holy Ghost not many days hence" (Acts 1:5 KJV). God said He will pour out His Spirit upon all flesh. I believe that day is coming soon.

"But ye shall receive power, after that the Holy Ghost is come upon you: and ye shall be witnesses unto me both in Jerusalem, and in all Judaea, and in Samaria, and unto the uttermost part of the earth" (Acts 1:8 KJV). When that day comes, we will be baptized in the Holy Spirit. We will be witnesses in our city, state, country, and around the world. You will share your testimony with everyone you meet. You will share the goodness of the Lord with them.

How will you know if you are filled with the Holy Spirit? There are twelve signs of the Holy Spirit's manifestation in your life:

1. Speaking in tongues: "And they were all filled with the Holy Ghost, and began to speak with other tongues, as the Spirit gave them utterance" (Acts 2:4 KJV). This was on the day of Pentecost, when they all were in unity and in one accord. The Holy Spirit was like a mighty rushing wind that came down from heaven, and it filled the entire room. Those gathered were able to speak in languages they had never spoken before.
2. Bearing the fruit of the Spirit: "But the fruit of the Spirit is love, joy, peace, longsuffering, gentleness, goodness, faith, Meekness, temperance: against such there is no law" (Galatians 5:22–23 KJV).

3. Singing hymns and psalms and making melody in your heart (Colossians 3:16, Ephesians 5:18–19).
4. Flowing rivers of living waters (John 7:38).
5. Praying in the Spirit (Ephesians 6:18, Jude 20).
6. Walking in the Spirit (Philippians 3:3).
7. Living in the Spirit (Romans 8:4, Galatians 5:25).
8. Baptized in the Holy Spirit (Acts 1:4).
9. Holy Spirit empowerment (Acts 1:8).
10. Spirit of wisdom (Ephesians 1:17).
11. Confession of Jesus Christ (1 John 4:2, 1 Timothy 3:16).
12. The gifts of the Holy Spirit (1 Corinthians 12:4–9). Stirring up the gifts, awakening those dormant gifts that have been lying dormant for too long.

After you repent and ask Jesus Christ to be your Lord and Savior and be baptized, your sins will be forgiven and you should automatically receive the Holy Spirit as a gift. "And Peter said to them, "Repent and be baptized every one of you in the name of Jesus Christ for the forgiveness of your sins, and you will receive the gift of the Holy Spirit. For the promise is for you and for your children and for all who are far off, everyone whom the Lord our God calls to himself" (Acts 2:38–39 KJV). God promised that you and your children will be saved if you only repent, give Him your sin, and are baptized in the Holy Spirit. Isn't that a great exchange? The only thing you have to do is to give Jesus your sins. Yes, turn them over to Him and believe in your heart, and you shall be saved. This is the beginning of an epic relationship with Jesus. Jesus will seal the deal by giving you the gift of the Holy Spirit. The Holy Spirit is your comforter and your help.

First Corinthians 12:4–11 talks about the varieties of gifts, but they all come from the same Spirit. There are varieties of service, but they come from the same Lord; to each is given gifts to demonstrate the manifestation of the Spirit for the common good of the church. The body of Christ will not lack anything. The Holy Spirit has graciously given the spiritual giant church body nine gifts that we should be operating in, which should flow down to the individual churches:

1. One is given through the Spirit the utterance of wisdom. We need this gift operating mightily in the church from the Holy Spirit more now than ever before. The church needs wisdom to guide us on how to handle various situations, such as school shootings. This hideous, unprecedented trend started nearly twenty years ago at Columbine High School in Colorado. The church needs wisdom about raising our children so that our children can make wise choices in life as they get older. The church needs wisdom about how to attack the prejudicial ignorance flowing through the land.

2. Another is given the utterance of knowledge. This goes without saying, but I would rather have a drop of God's knowledge than an ocean of knowledge from every man who has walked this earth. The gift of knowledge is called discernment. The church needs to know how to discern the spirit to determine if it is from God or the devil. If someone tells you in your mind to commit suicide, you need discernment to know which spirit it's coming from. You can rest assured that if someone is telling you to commit suicide, it is clearly nobody but the devil. The devil hates your guts and wants you dead. Jesus came to give you life more abundantly, and not to kill you. "The thief comes only to steal and kill and destroy. I came that they may have life and have it abundantly" (John 10:10 ESV). So for you to discern the spirit of suicide, you need to be awake and not sleepwalking in sin. Once you have been awakened, you need to rebuke and resist the devil. "Therefore, submit to God. But resist the Devil, and he will flee from you" (James 4:7 HCSB). Once you have resisted the devil, start drawing closer and closer to God. Then start telling yourself, "I choose life and not death. I speak life, and I refuse to commit suicide. My life is valuable and precious in God's eyes." Start telling yourself that you are beloved by the one who created you. Keep speaking life into your situation, by saying, "Jesus said He came to give me life and not to take my life, so I shall live and not die in Jesus's name." Tell the devil, "Jesus rebuked you over two thousand years ago. So go

back to hell where you belong and leave me alone, in Jesus's name." Remember that the devil tried to tempt Jesus into committing suicide at His vulnerable moment. "Then the devil took him to the holy city and set him on the pinnacle of the temple and said to him, "If you are the Son of God, throw yourself down, for it is written, "'He will command his angels concerning you,' and "'On their hands they will bear you up, lest you strike your foot against a stone'" (Matthew 4:5–6 KJV). How did Jesus respond to the devil? "Jesus said unto him, It is written again, Thou shalt not tempt the Lord thy God" (Matthew 4:7). So that should be your response to the devil when he tries to get you to commit suicide. God doesn't give us the big picture. That is His department. He gives us knowledge in parts.

3. Another is given faith by the same Spirit. The Bible tells us to walk by faith and not by sight. All we need is faith as small as a mustard seed.

4. Another is given the gift of healing. Now, the gift of healing is an awesome gift to have, because you can see people being healed right on the spot. You can witness people's limbs growing back, the blind being able to see, and the lame walking, instantly. If you are praying for someone to be healed from cancer, for example, and have faith even like the mustard seed and don't doubt, that person's faith should line up with your faith and they should be healed, if that is the will of the Father. How do you know the will of the Father when it comes to healing? Remember, we just talked about how the Spirit gives one the gift of wisdom, another gift of knowledge, and another gift of faith. So if you are walking in the Spirit, God will speak through the one with the gift of knowledge and tell him to go pray for the person with cancer. You with the knowledge will go and tell the ones with the gift of wisdom and faith to come with me. We can pray for this person who has cancer. God wants to heal them. They have to be obedient and lay hands on that person. When God tells you to move, you'd better be obedient and move. Now, God doesn't heal everyone, just like Jesus didn't heal everyone when He was walking on this earth. I do not know why He doesn't heal everyone, but what I do know

is that He heals. But even if the healing doesn't come, I am going to trust Him. If He chooses not to heal me on this side, I know I will be healed on the other side. So this is a win-win situation for you. When we are operating in the way the gifting flows, we know the body will not lack. The *Matthew Henry Commentary* discusses this: "Christ was bruised and crucified as a sacrifice for our sins, and by his stripes the diseases of our souls are cured." If you look up the definition of *healed* in the Merriam-Webster, Inc. dictionary on the Apple I-Tune App dated 2018, you'll see that it means to make sound or whole, to restore to original purity or integrity. By Jesus's stripes He wants to make us whole again. "He himself bore our sins in his body on the cross, that we might die to sin and live to righteousness. By his wounds you have been healed (1 Peter 2:24 ESV).

5. Another is given the gift of working miracles. Jesus performed miracles everywhere He went. Jesus said that we shall do greater work, so we should be seeing miracles happening everywhere we go.

6. Another is given the gift of prophecy. This is someone who can speak the truth into people's lives in love. How does the gift of prophecy works? You can meet a stranger and know absolutely nothing about them, and the Holy Spirit will reveal to you what they are going through. You know beyond a shadow of any doubt that this prophet is being used by God. Remember, a prophet prophesies in part. However, the Bible does warn us to beware of false prophets. That's why you need the gift of discerning the spirit. God gives us the wisdom to know the difference between a false prophet and His prophet.

7. Another is given the ability to distinguish between spirits. Discerning the spirit! Remember the woman who was bent over for eighteen years. Jesus saw the spirit of infirmity pressing down heavily on that woman, and she was healed instantly.

8. Another is given the gift of various kinds of tongues. That refers to prayer language that cannot be uttered.

9. Another is given the gift of the interpretation of tongues. This person has the capability to interpret what the spirit is saying.

All these gifts are empowered by the Holy Spirit for us to use them wisely and not abuse them. We have to be careful and not prostitute the gifts or sell them for profit. If you abuse them, they can be taken away from you. I believe that the body of Christ should be flowing influentially in the gifts, especially if you have received the Holy Spirit. If you are flowing mightily in one of those gifts that were given to you by the Holy Spirit, please ensure that you walk in love when you are ministering with them. If you are not walking in love, your words will sound like a clanging cymbal. You will just be making noise, without manifestation. I encourage you to read 1 Corinthians, chapters 12 through 14, for further knowledge of the gifts.

Please guard against envy over the gifts. It is easy to be jealous about someone else's gifts. When you see someone moving fluently in their gift, the devil will plant a thought in your head to make you think, *Why didn't God give me that gift?* Please be on your guard when it comes to the gifts. Remember, the Holy Spirit passes out the gifts, and I cannot dictate to Him that I want to pick another gift and not the one He gave me. It's the Holy Spirit's job to farm out the gifts, and not yours. Just be glad that you have one. Some people may have multiple gifts, because the Holy Spirit does not want the body of Christ lacking. Some people refuse to operate in the gifting. Some may not know if they have a gift. If you do not know which gift you should be operating in, ask the Holy Spirit. He will be glad to tell you. The primary gift I operate in is the gift of knowledge. I did not tell the Holy Spirit that is the gift I wanted. He freely gave it to me. God knows your makeup, because He created you. I'm a thinker. So I believe that is the reason why He gave me the gift of knowledge. I can sometimes operate in the gifts of wisdom, discernment, faith, and sometimes healing if I need to. But the gift of healing is my wife's gift, so I leave it to her. My wife cannot wait to see the manifestation of big miracles taking place in people's lives after she lays hands on them. My wife also operates in other gifts, such as discernment. She is very strong in that gift. I have a passion to see people set free from bondage. I understand that it is not me but the Holy Spirit who sets them free. I'm just a willing vessel who wants to be used mightily by God. So God knows which gift suits you. The gift that He gave you should fit like a glove. If you are a willing vessel, then He will activate the gifts He gave you.

~ TWENTY-NINE ~

Pouring Out the Holy Spirit

I strongly believe that we are in the last days and that God will be pouring out His Spirit upon all flesh. That son and daughter of yours that used to be a drunk, a drug addict, a liar, overtaken by greed, into prostitution, fornication, and heavy into pornography will be prophesying and seeing visions in the spirit realm. Your daughters you gave up on will be prophesying and praising the Lord in the Spirit. "And it shall come to pass in the last days, saith God, I will pour out of my Spirit upon all flesh: and your sons and your daughters shall prophesy, and your young men shall see visions, and your old men shall dream dreams" (Acts 2:17, KJV). Now when this happens, we will all see the great awakening that the church has been waiting for. Your children will be walking in the Spirit and no longer fulfilling the lust of the flesh. They will be in Christ, so their flesh will be crucified along with the affections and lusts. They will no longer be sleeping in sin. This will be another great awakening. "And they that are Christ's have crucified the flesh with the affections and lusts. If we live in the Spirit, let us also walk in the Spirit" (Galatians 5:24–25 KJV). You will experience like never before a healing in the land. God will heal all their diseases—not some of their diseases, but all of their diseases—on this great day of awakening. "Then he called his twelve disciples together, and gave them power and authority over all devils, and to cure diseases. And he sent them to preach the kingdom of God, and to heal the sick" (Luke 9:1–2 KJV).

"Now when the sun was setting, all they that had any sicknesses with diver's diseases brought them unto him; and he laid his hands on every one of them, and healed them. And devils also came out of many, crying out, and saying, Thou art Christ the Son of God. And he rebuking them suffered them not to speak: for they knew that he was Christ" (Luke 4:40–41 KJV).

"And God was doing extraordinary miracles by the hands of Paul, so that even handkerchiefs or aprons that had touched his skin were carried away to the sick, and their diseases left them and the evil spirits came out of them" (Acts 19:11–12 ESV). The Holy Spirit will bring special miracles by the hands of your sons and daughters. Someone who has a disease can just touch their skin and they will be healed from those evil spirits. That is the manifestation of the seal of the Holy Spirit resting mightily on them.

"But he was wounded for our transgressions, he was bruised for our iniquities: the chastisement of our peace was upon him; and with his stripes we are healed" (Isaiah 53:5 KJV).

In the day of the great awakening we will no longer go astray like lost sheep. "All we like sheep have gone astray; we have turned, every one, to his own way; and the Lord has laid on him the iniquity of us all" (Isaiah 53:6 ESV).

How do I know that this day is up on us? "Even on my male servants and female servants in those days I will pour out my Spirit, and they shall prophesy. And I will show wonders in the heavens above and signs on the earth below, blood, and fire, and vapor of smoke; the sun shall be turned to darkness and the moon to blood, before the day of the Lord comes, the great and magnificent day. And it shall come to pass that everyone who calls upon the name of the Lord shall be saved" (Acts 2:18–21 KJV). In verse 20 the sun shall be turned darkness and the moon to blood. In August 2017, the sun turned completely dark for a few minutes in some cities. Then in January 2018, we had a blood moon and a super moon. There is one part in those scriptures that has not happened yet: we have not seen the manifestation yet of God pouring out His Spirit upon all flesh. When that happens, we will know for certain that we are in the last days. Then everyone who calls upon the name of the Lord shall be saved. The only thing they need to say in those last days is "Jesus, save me," and they will be saved instantly.

I was talking with a friend of mine who told me that God told him that a famine is coming to the land. He asked, "What kind of famine?"

You probably were thinking, like I was, about lack of food. Right! God told him that this famine is the kind where the cost of a tomato will be five dollars and people won't be able to afford that. They will have to choose which sacrifices they are going to make: "Should we eat or pay our bills?" To keep from paying five dollars for a tomato, you might want to do your own gardening. God told him that it is time for His people to get out of debt. If a tomato will cost five dollars, just imagine how much your utility bill, bread, milk, and so on will cost.

God is going to set you free from the bondage the church has been in for decades. Do you know what the key will be that will set you free from those bondages? Repentance! Repentance is the key to opening the door of bondage and setting you free. Once the church has been awakened, we will repent and run back to our first love, who is Jesus Christ.

Through our awakening God is going to give His people 20-20 vision in the spirit realm. You are going to be able to see those things that are behind every decision. You are going to be able to silence the voice of the enemy and see those demons with a muzzle on their mouths. Hallelujah!

God is raising up an army of superheroes who will take back what is rightfully theirs. The kingdom of God suffers violence and from things being taken by force. "From the days of John the Baptist until now the kingdom of heaven has suffered violence, and the violent take it by force" (Matthew 11:12 ESV).

"I am writing to you, little children, because your sins are forgiven for his name's sake. I am writing to you, fathers, because you know him who is from the beginning. I am writing to you, young men, because you have overcome the evil one. I write to you, children, because you know the Father. I write to you, fathers, because you know him who is from the beginning. I write to you, young men, because you are strong, and the word of God abides in you, and you have overcome the evil one" (1 John 2:12–14 ESV).

When the church is strong in the Lord, you will be able to live a by-product or spin-off life that mimics Jesus Christ exclusively. He demonstrated that to us by showing us exactly how we should live a by-product life and not like in the days of Noah, Sodom and Gomorrah, and the five foolish virgins.

Once the church has experienced the great awakening, the hope of glory will rise in you. The church's hope should be built on nothing less than Jesus's blood and His righteousness. "For through the Spirit, by faith, we ourselves eagerly wait for the hope of righteousness" (Galatians 5:5 ESV). If the church has experienced the great awakening, we can wait for the hope of the returning of our Lord Jesus Christ to take us home: "waiting for our blessed hope, the appearing of the glory of our great God and Savior Jesus Christ" (Titus 2:13 ESV).

Endnotes

1   Statista: The Statistics Portal. https://www.statista.com. Accessed 3/18/18.

2   ABC News. https://www.abcnews.go.com. Accessed 3/18/18.

3   Stearns, Robert. *The Cry of Mordecai* (p. 28), publisher: Destiny Image Publishers, Inc. Shippensburg, PA. Copyright 2009

4   National Right to Life. "Abortion Statistics." https://www.nrlc.org/abortion/facts/abortionstats.html. Accessed 6/2/08.

5   National Right to Life. "Abortion in the U.S." https://www.nrlc.org/uploads/factsheets/FS01AbortionintheUS.pdf. Accessed 03/18/18.

6   Henry, Matthew. *Matthew Henry's Concise Commentary on the Whole Bible, from the Olive Tree Software Bible Study 6.*

7   Freedom Keys: Quotations. https://freedomkeys.com/quotations.htm

8   Henry, Matthew. *Matthew Henry's Concise Commentary on the Whole Bible, from the Olive Tree Software Bible Study 6.*

9   Ibid.

10 Ibid.

11 Good Reads. https://www.goodreads.com. Accessed 5/30/18.

12 Henry, Matthew. *Matthew Henry's Concise Commentary on the Whole Bible.*

13 Ibid.

14 Ibid.

15 Ibid.

16 Stearns, Robert. *The Cry of Mordecai* (p. 198); publisher: Destiny Image Publishers, Inc. Shippensburg, PA. Copyright 2009.

17 Henry, Matthew. *Matthew Henry's Concise Commentary on the Whole Bible, from the Olive Tree Software Bible Study 6.*

18 Stearns, Robert. *The Cry of Mordecai* (p. 32); publisher: Destiny Image Publishers, Inc. Shippensburg, PA. Copyright 2009.

19 Conner, Kevin J. *Interpreting the Symbols and Types* (p. 182); Published by City Bible Publishing, Portland, Oregon, Copyright 1992.

20 Stearns, Robert. *The Cry of Mordecai* (p. 198); publisher: Destiny Image Publishers, Inc. Shippensburg, PA. Copyright 2009.

21 Ibid. (p. 196).

22 Ibid.

23 Young, Sarah. *Jesus Calling: Enjoying Peace in His Presence* (p. 276).

24 Collins, Hakeem. *Heaven Declares: Prophetic Decrees to Start Your Day* (Day 68, pp. 2,463–66).

25 Ibid. (Day 83, p. 2,891).

26 Anne Graham Lotz's interview on the *Early Show*. http://www.prayerfoundation. org/billy_grahams_daughter.htm; Accessed online on 4/23/18.

27 Collins, Hakeem. *Heaven Declares: Prophetic Decrees to Start Your Day* (Day 75, pp. 2,659–63).

28 Henry, Matthew. *Matthew Henry's Concise Commentary on the Whole Bible, from the Olive Tree Software Bible Study 6.*

29 Collins, Hakeem. *Heaven Declares: Prophetic Decrees to Start Your Day* (Introduction, p. 319).

About the Author

Billy Driver lives with his wife, Anita, and son, David, in Huntsville, Alabama. Billy has been saved since the age of seventeen, and this is his first book. He has a passion to see people walking in victory and not in the devil's sleep in Sin Dungeon. He has served in prison ministry and is studying for a doctoral degree in theology.